House Beautiful
750
Decorating &
Design Ideas

House Beautiful
750
Decorating &
Design Ideas

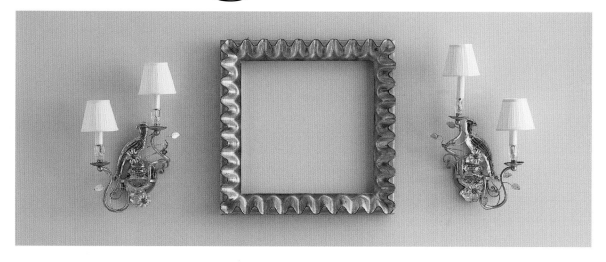

From The Editors of House Beautiful

HEARST BOOKS
A DIVISION OF STERLING PUBLISHING CO., INC.

Library of Congress Cataloging-in-Publication Data

House beautiful 750 decorating & design ideas : express yourself with color, pattern, light & style / from the editors of House Beautiful.
      p. cm.
  ISBN 1-58816-269-9
  1. Interior decoration--United States--History--20th century. I.
Title: 750 decorating & design ideas. II. Title: Seven hundred fifty decorating and design ideas. III. House beautiful.
  NK2115.H545 2003
  747--dc21
                            2003007715

10 9 8 7 6 5 4 3 2

Published by Hearst Books
A Division of Sterling Publishing Co., Inc.
387 Park Avenue South, New York, NY 10016

House Beautiful and Hearst Books are trademarks owned by
Hearst Magazines Property, Inc., in USA, and Hearst Communications, Inc., in Canada.

www.housebeautiful.com

Distributed in Canada by Sterling Publishing
C/o Canadian Manda Group, One Atlantic Avenue, Suite 105
Toronto, Ontario, Canada M6K 3E7

Distributed in Australia by Capricorn Link (Australia) Pty. Ltd.
P.O. Box 704, Windsor, NSW 2756 Australia

Edited by Pamela Horn

Printed in China

ISBN 1-58816-269-9

Contents

Introduction

Decorating, in all of its elements—from paint color to furnishings, accessories and fabrics—is a decidedly personal experience. At House Beautiful, we are flooded with letters from readers asking for advice on every conceivable area of decorating. Some of them have very specific questions such as the choice of a particular window treatment, or the choice of art over a mantel. Others want more general advice on how to accessorize or how to punch up a neutral room with color. What strikes me about all of these inquiries is that they are from the heart. We care deeply about our houses, and all of us enjoy new ideas and advice.

But so much of the time, we take those ideas and that advice in small doses—often so narrowly focused that we don't get the complete picture of how to decorate our homes. That's why this book, *House Beautiful 750 Decorating & Design Ideas*, is so unique and exciting. Here, in one place, you'll find practical ideas for every aspect of decorating. After all, the overwhelming majority of Americans who care about their interiors cannot afford the fees charged by decorators and consultants. Yet, the quality of free design advice, as you'll see in this book, has never been better. Add that to the fact that retailers out there like Target, Crate & Barrel, Pottery Barn, Restoration Hardware and others have brought great furnishings to the masses at much lower prices than those charged at trade-only showrooms, through designers. Great style and design are now available to virtually anyone who has the interest to look for it all, and that means millions of people. Young people, for instance, are more interested in the look of their own rooms than their parents were at the same age a generation ago. And parents are more interested in changing their decor than their own parents were. Remember when living rooms were virtually unused, almost museum-like areas where no one dared go? Remember when kitchens were an afterthought? Remember when people bought whole suites of bedroom furniture, for instance, instead of mixing and matching like today?

Design for the 21st Century is here. In this book, you will find chapters devoted to color, lighting, storage, accessorizing, entertaining, and choices for the walls, windows, and floors. Not all of our tastes and styles are the same, so in one chapter you might respond to advice on a neutral palette while others want advice on how to splash a room with color. There is nothing contradictory about this: We simply are not all cut from the same mold, thankfully.

As a design magazine editor, I love the fact that on any given day, I can walk into a very traditional house and the next day I find myself in a modern house that might as well be battery operated with color. But there are some underlying rules that do tend to bind us all together. Good taste knows no one style but it certainly makes the difference in a well-decorated room and a room we'd all rather not visit. But all of us need help sometimes in using our personal tastes in a way that is functional for not only us, but also our family and our guests. Consider Idea Number 173, for instance, in this book: "Store more. Bookshelves above or around your desk will keep the materials you need within arms reach but off the work surface." Simple advice but it makes a big difference when someone walks in your room and sees things orderly, and not cluttered and messy.

Or, even more simple, is Idea Number 422: "Paint your front door." How long has it been since you did that? It makes an immediate difference to guests who arrive at your house, yet few of us think about our front doors very often.

I hope you enjoy this book and learn as much as I have in reading it.

—MARK MAYFIELD
Editor-in-Chief

Colors & Patterns

Color sets a mood. So much has been written about color, its psychology, and power. Color can be introduced into a room in a variety of ways—from paint to fabric to an infinite number of decorative details such as paintings, wallpaper, window treatments, furniture, art and collections. It can make a room more cozy or airy—larger or smaller. Rooms can feel more energetic, serene, casual, or formal through the use of colors and patterns. With so many possibilities about where to use color in a room, and with the multitude of colors on the charts, it is easy to become confused and discouraged. The most persuasive argument about use of color, however, remains personal preference. Use the following tips to make color an element of beauty and self-expression in your home decorating.

Tips to Color Up Your Life

1 Blue and blue-and-white rooms are generally fresher, cooler and more serene than rooms colored from opposite ends of the color wheel. That's why you see so many beach houses decorated in soothing blue and white.

2 Red, purple, orange, peach, brick, ocher, and yellow are ideal for warming up spaces in cold climates, rooms without impressive architectural features, and spatially challenged apartments in urban centers. Warmer tones make rooms seem more livable.

There is no such thing as a bad color, just bad combinations. Avocado green looks splendid with a dose of off-white trim and maybe a pale peach or soft aqua pillow. Baby pink looks all grown up when mated with a rich chocolate brown. Turquoise can be magical with a dash of coral, a bit of gold, and a pinch of black.

Ceilings will appear higher if you paint them pale shell pink or creamy white. Silver-leafed or high-gloss lacquered finishes also add ceiling height.

If your room is small, all four walls should be the same color. In large rooms (in which the walls are more than 20 feet long), you can get away with un-identical walls, but try to stick with different tones of the same color.

Remember to mix and not necessarily match, colors, and avoid mélanges that look too strange or forced.

If you love white walls, choose paint with a good chalky matte finish and then tinge it with a little something extra: add a bit of yellow or lavender to the mix for a hint of depth and sophistication.

Beige linen or silk upholstery and curtains look more exciting and polished if you add coral or periwinkle blue trim.

You can mix three, four, or even five gem-toned upholstered pieces in the same room. Armchairs, ottomans, sofa pillows, side chairs, sofas, and even curtains covered in glistening raw silk in shades of sapphire blue, ruby red, emerald green, topaz yellow, and citrine green harmonize beautifully.

Before beginning any decorating project involving color, think seriously about your gut reactions to it. What hues please you the most?

After settling on a color, determine which tint or shade you want. Tint: the color plus white. Shade: the color plus black. Then decide on how saturated the color should be.

Use plenty of white, whether in a striped fabric or for upholstery piping—bright colors lose their punch next to beige or taupe.

The primary colors are red, blue, and yellow. Their complementary secondary colors are green, orange, and purple, respectively. All colors are based on combinations with primary colors.

If you are thinking of painting your bedroom an offbeat color, get a set of sheets in that shade and live with them awhile first. The same goes for the bathroom—test-drive new colors with a towel or two. Don't re-cover all of your furniture in a saturated tone you're not sure about; try slipcovers instead.

Work with several colors at once. Stripes,

tartans, tattersalls, and checks help you

achieve an exuberant yet graphic unified

look—they are patterns that men, women,

and children can agree on.

Chocolate brown on living room walls

really makes all the whites—and the

art—pop in a room.

Learn to Be a Pro with Patterns

17 Patterns add dash to a room and contrast with solids. Use them but be conscious about whether they distract from the beauty of furniture and walls.

18 Use prints on pieces that are prone to get dirty.

19 Big florals, plaids, and stripes on a patterned rug are a mistake.

20 Ideal patterns for draperies and upholstery are translucent tone-on-tone prints.

The Lowdown on Upholstery

21 When you fall in love with a piece of upholstered furniture, it's easy to forget the fundamentals. So keep the three "f"s, explained below, in mind, and buy the highest quality you can afford. It's an investment that can be re-built, re-padded, and re-covered.

22 Frame: Look for those made of hardwoods with a dense grain, such as ash, maple, walnut, and oak. Nonwarping kiln-dried frames are top of the line. Frame joints should be secured with dowels and glue for the strongest grip.

23 Filling: ask about the springs. Find out if the piece of furniture has eight-way hand-tied coils; these provide the best support. Prefabricated springs inserted into the frame are a moderately priced option. Side-by-side zigzag wires are the least comfortable and least expensive choice. In cushions, density equals quality. Options include all down, a foam center wrapped with down, a down and synthetic fiberfill blend, or fiberfill only.

24 Fabric: Be sure the pattern on the seat-cushion lines up with the upholstered frame. Welts should be even; skirts should be lined. Look for neat, tight tailoring.

When upholstering with patterns remember that prints look best on simple graphic shapes with exposed legs.

In the living room, fauteuils make a lovely frame for prints.

A sofa looks less rigid with a subtle large-scale print on the seat and back cushions and the body in solid.

In the bedroom use a soft print for walls and curtains.

Major mistakes with patterns usually occur in scale. A pattern's size greatly affects color and shape.

A bed can be dreamy with a bedspread in transparent patterns.

Never ever use too many florals and plaids in the same area or disparate, jarring prints in one room.

Never ever use large patterns on delicate furniture.

Fabric Shopping Tips

33 Choosing fabrics is most people's favorite part of the decorating process. Fortunately, sources for fabrics abound; they include:

34 To-the-trade-only showrooms: Purveyors of fabrics (and usually wall coverings) available only to those customers working with a designer or architect with whom the firm has an account. Some retail stores offer "decorator services" which permit you access to these showrooms through their personnel.

35 Fabric outlets: Fabric manufacturers at these locations offer discontinued patterns, overruns, and remainders at substantial savings. Ask to see the entire length of fabric you wish to buy so that you can check for flaws. If you pay in cash, you might get a further discount.

36 Furniture showrooms: These retailers offer a selection of fabrics at varying price and quality levels for the upholstered pieces they sell. If you don't like any of the fabrics offered, you can provide your own (C.O.M., or customer's own material). Be sure to know the width of the fabric and that of its repeat when speaking to the salesperson. He or she will be able to tell you exactly how much fabric will be required.

Beyond the Pale— In Need of a Room Quick Fix?

37

Learn about colors and mix your own paint. Use a brush rather than a roller for a bit of texture.

A room looks instantly rich when you cover the walls in fabric, even if it only costs $5.00 a yard.

An ordinary chair looks
better the minute you
stain or paint it black.

Collect bits of antique
silk and ribbon to trim
chairs, pillows and nap-
kins.

Cream lampshades are
dull. Cover the shade
with patterned fabric for
a warmer look.

Texture Adds Depth to a Room

42 Paint offers limitless opportunities to add artistic flair to furniture and rooms.

43 Patterned walls, interesting fabrics, and a multitude of materials all give rich complexity to a room.

44 When it comes to furniture, applying a coat of paint is the perfect way to make new out of old.

45 A fresh finish may disguise rings, scratches and nicks to a second-hand piece of furniture but won't correct larger structural problems such as poorly aligned drawers and wobbly legs.

Marbleizing or marbling is a decorative technique where paints are blended, mottled and streaked, with a sponge or feather, to make the surface appear like marble.

Treating doors, chests, walls, and floors with

colors and special paint techniques are ways

to heighten the complexity of a room.

Playing with Pastels

48 On a wall or sofa, a soft pastel subtly seduces the eye and warms up a room. When used in unexpected combinations, pastels can also be quite arresting.

49 Pastels are an effective use of color as they often provide definitions to surfaces and furniture that white paint or fabric cannot achieve.

Pastels can infuse walls, furniture, art, and a

rug and still not give the feeling of excess.

Instead of using conventional choices such as pink or baby blue, it is more striking and interesting to use a pairing of periwinkle and pistachio green.

Depending upon the tone of the color, paler pine and birch may be better materials to use in rooms with pastels. Mahogany furniture might simply overpower the softer colors.

You only have to look to your garden in the spring for inspiration to find shades of atmospheric pastels in pinks, lavenders, the palest blues, and delicate washes of green.

When a Splash of Color Makes the Difference

Sometimes a brush with color on a piece of fabric or furniture is all it takes to bring a room to life.

Painting a flea-market find or unfinished piece of pine offers an opportunity for creative expression.

Mustard, barn red, gray, faded teal, or dull green are authentic colonial colors. These as well as other period colors often come ready mixed from paint companies.

Still lifes in paintings and real flowers are

another way to infuse color into neutral spaces.

Patterns and colors work in layers, but sometimes it takes one bold shock of color to make a real statement in a room!

Every Room in the House

Each room in the house has its own special personality. It is in the details that a room truly comes together. The most important part about designing, renovating, or enhancing a room is to ask what you need and find practical and beautiful tips that will achieve your goal. You have to pay attention to the obvious as well as to the subtle. One universal notion that runs through decorating every room in your house is balance. Balance your goals with your limitations; balance your budget with your fantasies—then your design decisions will reflect your needs and your own personal sense of style.

Bored with Your Bedroom?

Here are the Nuts and Bolts of Headboards

Guest rooms

are the place to

take risks: bright

colors make

houseguests

happy.

The bed is the focal point of the bedroom so an upholstered headboard makes a statement and offers limitless opportunities for design.

A queen size headboard will attach easily to a standard metal frame for a mattress and box spring.

If you think up an unusual headboard style, have your workroom make a template of the shape so you can be sure it works.

If you redecorate frequently, slipcover your headboards.

Today's mattress sets are often extra thick. Before ordering a custom headboard, measure the height from the floor to the top of your mattress so that your workroom can get the right proportions.

How to Decorate a Woman's Dressing Room

Create a serene, roman-
tic space with mirrors
with painted trim and
fresh flowers on the
dressing table.

The chair should be a very
girly shape with painted
legs and plain fabric.

Great embellishments are
an ottoman, a crisp chair,
a floor lamp, and a cabi-
net with glass doors.

Use an antique chest or
dresser.

The palette should be ivory or beige as it

shows off the subtleties of what you are

wearing.

Three-way folding mirrors and slightly antiqued silver mirrors are loveliest.

Shaded lamps give soft, flattering light.

Use wall-to-wall carpeting or a lovely wool-and-silk area rug.

Walls should have simple paint or wallpaper, but no wild graphic patterns.

The windows should have simple draperies with soft sheers for privacy.

Line cupboards with wallpaper; stack clothes neatly and top with a sachet.

Put out a beautiful clock, crystal jars, and a modern silver tray.

Put cosmetics in pullout drawers so that you can see everything at once.

Use fabric-lined baskets for accessories.

Hang a pretty chandelier.

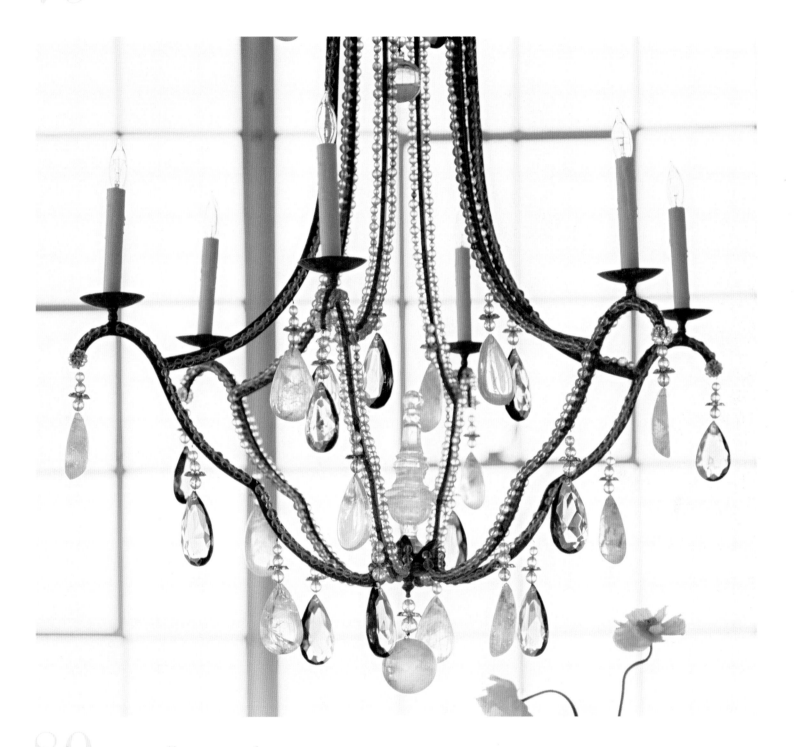

Find ways to really personalize your

space by using unexpected elements for

decoration. If you are crazy for hats,

display your collection!

How to Get Romantic in Your Bedroom

81

Blue is the safest color for a bedroom. It's very relaxing, and it appeals to both men and women. Yellow is very stimulating and pink sometimes has a candy-box effect.

82

Never leave the box spring as is; cover it with a mattress pad trimmed with antique or new lace. For cleaning purposes you can even attach the trim with Velcro, so you don't have to re-stitch it every time you launder the cover.

Set off the predominant color with contrasting furniture and accessories. For example, a desk and chair of beautiful wood enhances a palette.

84

Use birds-in-ruins blue toile pattern every-where from the walls to the lampshade to the bed skirt.

A large down-filled bolster gives wonderful support for your pillows, of which there should be many. Keep extra pillows in an inexpensive wicker basket near the bed, and dress it up with paint to match your surroundings.

Achieve the eternal romance of a four-poster bed without the heaviness by creating a corona. You can make one by suspending a wicker basket upside down from the ceiling, then hang white linen from that. Another option is to cover metal tubing with fabric to create a kind of cage to support your bed curtains.

Upholster your walls—the batting underneath creates a sound cocoon that's invaluable in such a private space.

Place a featherbed on top of the mattress. It gives you an added soft layer and makes you feel like the princess in The Princess and the Pea.

Stay with natural fibers: sleep on cotton, silk, or linen sheets.

For elegance and drama paint your ceiling gold.

Fragrance is important throughout your bedroom—use little antique needlework bags filled with potpourri on your bedside tables.

A settee or a pair of comfortable chairs at the foot of the bed are a good idea so one person can watch TV or read before retiring.

Don't leave bedside tables bare. Top them

with glass so that you can place things on

top. Dress the tables up with embroidered or

lace-trimmed fabric.

A lovely break-

fast tray or

workbasket

handily turns

the bed into a

makeshift dining

room or office.

Start
From the
Drawing
Board and
Make the
Kitchen
Uniquely
Yours . . .

Function &
Efficiency

As you plan your kitchen,
consider your own work
habits and preferences:
where do you stand or sit
when you do certain
chores? Is meal prepara-
tion a solo or a shared
activity? This will inform
the size of "traffic lanes"
you will need. Leave about
3½ to 4 feet between the
counter and an island.

If you are fortunate enough to have the room, include two islands in your kitchen plan—one dedicated to prep space, the other reserved for dining. Such an arrangement gives guests a place to sit and chat with the cook without being underfoot.

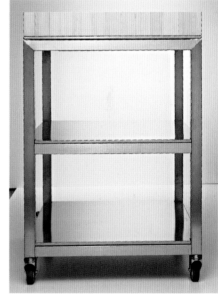

If you like the ideas of an island but would prefer to keep the center space open, consider a commercial-style stainless steel island on locking casters. You can roll it out when you need it and push it out of the way when you don't.

The side of an island may be customized with storage shelves to display books, collectibles, or vases.

Although islands can be large and rectangular, they can also be free form, and a combination of shapes, levels, and surfaces. Some angle through a room, situating various prep areas across from workspace along the wall, while others resemble old-fashioned pine kitchen tables, displaying beautifully shaped legs.

Be sure to specify a prep surface that's 37 to 38 inches high (the standard is 36 inches), which professionals consider a more comfortable working height.

If yours is a two-cook kitchen, or if children like to help out at mealtimes, think about creating multiple work areas that allow users to go from separate sinks to the refrigerator without crossing one another's paths.

No one wants to carry hot dishes far, so be sure to provide a heat-resistant landing area next to the stove where you can set down dishes coming off the cooktop or out of the oven.

Planning where your water sources will be is important. Separate sinks in the main preparation and cleanup areas will keep raw foods and dirty dishes safely apart. If you prepare pasta or soups frequently, consider an above-range faucet for filling large stockpots.

Also think about including in your plan a compartmentalized sink that lets you separate items. Outfit a sink with a sliding cutting board so you can chop vegetables right where you're washing them, then sponge scraps into the sink.

A desk in the kitchen can be a simple space, handy for planning menus and paying bills, or it can be more elaborate with a computer, TV, and stereo.

106

In most kitchens, the trash is located near the sink. Install a pullout trash bin near the prep area so you can push scraps directly from the counter into the bin.

107

If you enter the kitchen directly from outside or the garage, place some hooks and a storage bench for boots. You'll avoid tracking in dirt and clutter. This is also a good place for a message board.

108

If there is a sunny window in your main prep area, keep the glare factor in mind when choosing surfaces. Avoid those that will reflect sunlight into your eyes. Use window treatments to help block the sunlight.

109

Given the heavy traffic through most kitchens, opt for flooring that has a subtle pattern like speckles. It will be far more forgiving of day-to-day use.

Mixing counter surfaces can be incredibly practical as well as a dramatic design statement. Try, for instance, an area of granite surrounding a stainless-steel sink set in a butcher-block counter. This looks beautiful, and also catches splashes of water that could eventually mar the wood.

If you like to work directly on your countertop, choose a solid surfacing material that won't show cuts and nicks—consider butcher block and granite.

Reserve tiles for walls or counters that receive light use. Laminates provide a broad range of patterns and colors at a reasonable cost. To protect them from hot pots and sharp knives, keep portable cutting boards on hand.

Durable stainless steel countertops are another way to go. If the cost is too high, consider a small accent counter instead.

114 When deciding on floors, the softer on the feet the better! Vinyl, cork, and rubber tiles are more forgiving when things are dropped and easier on the back than harder surfaces.

115 Wood floors are also resilient. If properly sealed they clean up easily with a damp mop. Also, check out bamboo flooring for its appealing looks and eco-friendly nature.

116 Consider poured cement floors and counters. It is virtually nonporous, bacteria-resistant, and seamless, all of which make it very sanitary. This material can also be custom colored.

117 Be aware of acoustics as you choose surfaces. A large room with many hard materials will increase the amount of noise. Sound-absorbing surfaces, such as fabric window treatments and area rugs in dining spaces, can help reduce the noise factor.

118 Installing a narrow cabinet on the dining room side of a divider lets you store dishes where they are needed.

If you want a walk-in pantry but don't have the space, here is an efficient, space-saving alternative: one or two narrow pullout pantry units that blend with your cabinets. That way staples and kids' snacks and cereals will be within easy view and reach.

Under-counter cabinets (including corner units) that function as drawers, or have pullout wood or wire storage drawers or shelves, will make items that usually get lost, easy to find and retrieve. Pullouts are especially useful in narrow cabinets, which can be customized to store trays, baking sheets, and cutting boards upright.

Get rid of cabinet clutter by building in custom drawers designed to hold spices, canned goods, and utensils.

Touch-latch cabinet doors or easy-to-grasp pulls provide easy access to everyone, including people whose grip is weak. Also be sure drawers slide easily.

123

If you have a large family or entertain frequently, don't be afraid to double up on an appliance. Two dishwashers may be helpful for separating dishes from utensils or for a quick cleanup during a party.

124

Tile and stone floors have an unmistakable beauty and come in many colors and designs. If you love that look but want softer flooring, consider integrating tile or stone into another surface. Try creating a border or an accent design to delineate or highlight areas—but make sure there is a level transition between materials for safety's sake.

Glass-fronted cabinet doors can increase the feeling of spaciousness in a room. Try using textured or opaque glass panels to give a sense of depth while obscuring the contents.

As you design your kitchen, remember that placement can affect the efficiency of your appliances. A refrigerator's compressor will work harder if the refrigerator sits in direct sunlight or near a hot appliance.

A laundry room in or near your kitchen can be very efficient. Stackable units are easily concealed behind louvered doors or door fronts to match cabinets.

Serious party-givers or wine-lovers don't need to store wines in the cellar or a dark corner. Various coolers range from compact under-the-counter units to refrigerator height models that hold upward of 150 bottles.

Rounded or bull-nose corners and edges on countertops might lessen the severity of nasty bumps and bruises, especially if you've got young children whose heads are about counter height. You can also select appliances that have controlled lock-outs so they're off-limits to the little ones.

Augment daytime sunny spots with supplemental lighting—dimmers can adjust the light to accommodate users. Maximize your lighting's effectiveness by installing separate controls for general, task, and accent lighting.

To highlight work areas use a combination of direct over-the-counter and under-the-cabinet task lighting. Soften the impact of the latter by placing the light behind the valance (the lip on the cabinet's front) and directing beams toward the wall.

Be sure there is lighting under the range hood so that you can see what you're cooking.

Pendant lights are a beautiful design statement that also direct the light exactly where you need it. Use fixtures to repeat dominant shapes or accent colors.

Be creative with glass blocks: Install them in small areas, along other windows, or as design accents to let in light without sacrificing privacy.

Create a custom look for your range hood by finishing or facing it to blend with adjacent cabinets. If the hood will hang over a center island, choose a unit with a striking shape or one made of a particularly beautiful material like copper. Make sure that the hood is wider than your stove or cooktop, extending about 6 inches per side.

The demand for residential stoves, cooktops, and ovens that mimic commercial units is increasing. Convection ovens keep air moving to eliminate hot spots; steam ovens keep baked foods moist; rotisseries let you slow roast; while infrared broilers caramelize the surfaces of meats and vegetables. Visiting websites and show rooms that keep pace with these culinary trends will help you find equipment to suit your needs.

Corner windows and sky-lights placed high on a pitched ceiling can make small rooms look larger.

Use cooler-burning fluorescent lights, available in flattering warm tones, for under-cabinet task lighting. Halogens can heat up overhead cabinets and cause oils and grains stored there to turn rancid.

Bold color, even in a small kitchen, can be a big design plus. If you paint one wall lemon yellow, a room filled with natural sunlight will appear even sunnier.

Design an island with cabinets that are a different color than the other cabinets.

Installing a plug mold—a row of outlets that looks like a track—underneath cabinets lets you plug in appliances anywhere along your counter. It also ensures that outlets don't interfere with the designs of tiles and wallpaper.

Tame refrigerator-art clutter with a row or entire wall of simple frames. Use them to display the ever-changing children's artwork that passes through your kitchen.

Make a bold design statement by using two different colors on cabinets, particularly when cabinetry is used to separate the kitchen from the dining area. The consistency in cabinet style will keep the entire space unified; the second color on the divider cabinetry will create a visual break and delineate areas or use.

Quick Fixes for the Kitchen

Replace the hardware. Spruce up your drawers and cabinets by changing the hardware. Hardware comes in unique designs and finishes from a variety of outlets.

Install a new faucet. A new faucet can bring a fresh look to an old sink. Although replacing one is not a large project, it can be time consuming. Consider hiring a plumber to do the installation.

Lay a vinyl floor. The floor is one of the largest expanses in the kitchen, so a new look here can provide a refreshing facelift.

Add a backsplash. A tile backsplash behind

your sink, counter, or range looks great and

will last longer than either paint or wallpaper.

Change the lighting. Changing the ceiling fixture can create a whole new look.

Paint. A couple of gallons of a fresh hue are sometimes all a kitchen needs. Consider paint that has an eggshell or semigloss finish instead of a flat one; it resists staining better and wipes up more easily.

Hang a wallpaper border to add a personal touch. To make quick work of this project, opt for a border with a peel-and-stick back.

Install window treatments to warm up the look of the room. Many stores sell curtains, but you might want to hang a vintage apron or dishtowel instead. Just make sure that whatever you hang is washable; items in the kitchen need regular cleaning.

Make your kitchen far more functional and welcoming by putting it in order. To help in the process, look for specialized storage products: you'll find more than you could possibly dream up. Consider the following: racks to hold lids for pots and pans inside a cabinet door, pullout racks that install on cabinet shelves, and bread boxes that fit in draws.

Use recycling bins—this will help clutter-proof your kitchen and keep it clean.

Ways to Enhance Your Bathroom

Showers

Stone, slate, marble, ceramic, or glass floor and wall tiles in the shower are the best ways to go. They last longer and clean up better than other materials.

When you install or replace a showerhead, the tallest member of your family should stand in the stall or tub so that you can determine where the showerhead should be positioned.

Tubs

If you buy an antique claw-foot tub, check to see that all your four feet are intact and firmly attached. (Repairs on old tubs and hardware can be tricky and costly.)

Install a hotel towel rack above your tub; it will make room for storage space elsewhere.

Consider investing in a new tub rather than using a spray-on chemical treatment on an old one; it won't last!

Sinks

Pedestal sinks look stylish and strong, but they eat up storage space. A skirted sink—or a sink set into a counter space and cabinets—is more practical in a tiny bathroom.

Quick Fixes

160

If your budget doesn't allow for a total bath redo, replace your hardware. Chrome, brass, pewter, and nickel are like good jewelry on a plain dress.

161

A dark, windowless bathroom should be kept light and bright: stick to white and shiny pastel colors.

Mirrors

162

Don't cover a wall with a big slab of mirror: a large framed mirror, or several smaller ones hung on walls or even propped up on the floor, are much more attractive and easier to clean.

163

Magnifying mirrors are a must; they work best when attached to metal accordion-style arms located to one side of your medicine cabinet. Choose a quality swing-arm mirror that can take a lot of wear and tear.

Make sure your mirrors are beveled, which gives them a more finished, decorated look.

Toilets

If you live in an older apartment building or house and you are replacing your toilets, make sure to measure, measure, measure. Many of the new toilets are too large for old bathrooms.

Color & Accessories

Select white tile, toilets, tubs, and sinks, and your bathroom will not date. Inject color through painted or papered walls, shower curtains, window treatments, and towels.

Keep the knickknacks to a minimum. A profusion of doodads leaves a large bathroom without focus and a small bathroom cluttered and cramped.

Hang pictures on the walls—they add a charming and friendly note.

Plastic shower curtains are clingy and not very fresh, whereas natural fiber shower curtains are simple to launder; "easy glide" ball bearing chrome hooks facilitate opening and closing.

If you desire a small area rug, consider hemp: it doesn't attract mildew, and it's strong enough to with-stand frequent laundering.

Home
Office
Ideas

171 Set up shop—somewhere. Shared spaces make up 58 percent of the home offices in the country, with 33 percent located in the bedrooms; 15 percent in the den or a great room; 12 percent in the dining room; 10 percent in the living room; 9 percent in the kitchen; 6 percent in the basement; and the remainder in other rooms.

172 Your home office should feel like "command central" with everything you need within easy reach.

Store more. Bookshelves above or around

your desk will keep the materials you need

within arm's reach but off the work surface.

174 Add on. If your budget permits, build an office addition—you might be able to recoup as much as 70 percent of the cost of the project at resale.

175 Consider your clients. If you expect clients to visit regularly, try to set your office apart from the home as much as possible. A separate entrance to your office, if you can have one, creates an aura of professionalism.

176 Wake up your bedroom. A bedroom usually offers lots of natural light, good ventilation, heat and air conditioning, and electrical power. But consider your partner: If your work requires you to burn the midnight oil, locate your office somewhere else.

177 Go underground. The most ideal situation is a walk-out basement that opens to grade since this type of space provides an outside entrance. Claim neglected space.

Get up to the attic. But before moving your office upstairs, check that the space is adequately ventilated and insulated and can be equipped with phone and power outlets. You may need to consider installing skylights to admit natural light.

Use what's there. The size and shape of your office, and the furniture you already own, will have much to do with determining the layout of your office. Take these elements into account, then pick a layout that will play off their strengths: A U-shaped work area will allow you to keep everything within reach on three surfaces; an L-shaped work area offers the advantage of getting equipment off your desk and onto a secondary surface without taking up as much room as a U; and a parallel layout lets you move between two surfaces placed opposite each other.

Try to stay out of the kitchen. Although many bright ideas are cooked up at the kitchen table, experts warn that this space is too distracting to make a good office location.

Commandeer the closet. Creating an office in a closet can be a lifesaver for the space-challenged. File cabinets can support a work surface, and upper walls are ideal for strong shelves.

Grab the garage. If you live in a warm climate you can keep the car outside and transform the garage into a home office.

If your office does double duty—as a den, say—you can't take a deduction for any office-related expenses.

Beware of glare. Make sure your computer screen is placed to avoid glare, either facing a wall without a window or at a right angle to a window. Curtains or blinds will also help.

Remember clearance. Drawers are made to be opened, so allow 24 inches of clearance in front of the file cabinets.

Spend—and save—smart. Think about what drives your business. If technology is key, invest in equipment and keep furniture costs down. If clients visit, devote dollars to furniture and design.

187 Measure. It seems obvious, but many eager consumers buy furniture without measuring their room first.

188 Pick a winning workstation. The type you choose depends on your work style. If you like lots of room to spread out, look for a station with a large top surface. If you like everything neatly stowed away, opt for a piece with plenty of storage.

189 Save space with an armoire. You can store your computer and other electronic equipment in it, and when you are finished with your workday, just close your "office" doors.

190 Get your clothes out of the closet. If you don't have enough wall space for bookcases, take out the closet's spare rods and build shelves top to bottom to store work materials.

191 Pay attention to your chair. Do not skimp on a bargain chair—buy an ergonomic seat.

Think modular. If you expect your office to expand eventually, look for modular pieces. Look for furniture manufactured with casters for mobility.

Let the Web work for you. The Internet is an easy way to preview products without visiting every furniture store in town. If you feel confident enough to buy online, stick to ready-to-assemble furniture, which costs less to ship because it comes in a flat box.

Keep quality in mind. When you're in a furniture store, check all moving parts—drawers, keyboard trays, and doors. And if you are purchasing a product over the Internet, find out about the materials and construction details before you make your decision.

Set the tone with color. Generally speaking, cool colors, such as green and blue, produce a calming effect. Don't feel you have to stick to the standard corporate gray: Bright accents (as long as they're not overwhelming) can create an impression of energy and creativity and keep the space inviting, as well.

Keep it personal. A home office should have

an aesthetic that reflects the interests of the

user. Visitors can get a sense of who you are.

Be good to your body. To avoid physical stress, make sure that the furniture you choose is ergonomically correct. Look for adjustable features that will allow you to change the alignment of your keyboard tray, monitor stand, and footrest.

Check your power requirements. Make sure your home office has the necessary power outlets and wiring to run your technology. If you are setting up in an old home office where wiring needs to be retrofitted, consult an electrician.

Get connected. Select a phone that is comfortable for business use, ideally one with multiple lines and voice mail. Phones with headsets allow you to keep your hands free to type or write.

Look to the future. By keeping up to date with developing technology, you'll be able to anticipate your future needs.

Consider style. If your office is in a shared room, you may want to choose office pieces that will complement the existing furnishings.

Think before you buy. Consider what types of activities your work entails before heading to the furniture store. Will you be sitting at a computer? Meeting with clients? Assembling and shipping a product?

Before purchasing expensive electronics, figure out how much space you have available.

Get a guarantee. Equipment failure can have a serious impact on your business, so make sure you know the terms of your service agreement.

Install a backup system. Don't risk losing your files if your computer fails. Use removable media drives or external hard drives to back up data.

Conserve paper. Use a scanner, and then store information of all types— from invoices to business cards—electronically.

For now, keep wires under control. Most new home office furniture has built-in wire management systems that keep wires out of sight. You can also buy tubes and spools to keep wires neat.

Analyze your systems. You can have all the technology you need, great furniture, and a beautiful decorating scheme, but if you don't have any systems for organizing incoming information, you'll end up with piles of stuff everywhere. Designate one area for reading materials, using stacking bins or decorative wicker baskets to hold them.

Pare down your periodicals. Once a week, get rid of old publications. Tear out articles of interest and file them. Keep in mind that many back issues are available on the Internet.

Keep the writing on the wall. Dry eraser boards—smooth white boards that you can write on with markers, then wipe clean—are a great way to track projects. Old-fashioned bulletin boards can also come in handy to keep information in easy view.

Invest in your printer. Remember that the documents you generate represent your business, so spend the extra money on a high-quality printer.

Save space with multifunctional units. Most people don't have room for four or five separate pieces of equipment—fax, scanner, answering machine, etc. Keep in mind, however, that if one function fails, you might have to replace the entire unit.

Innovative Ideas for Fireplaces

213

Try the unexpected: a sleek streamlined mantel next to a traditional dining room table and chairs. Your fireplace will really jump!

214

Storage of firewood comes in many forms. When no built-in storage exists, other solutions can be devised: stacking on the hearth, piling in buckets, or standing in pails.

215
White paint on an old brick fireplace can subtract years from its age.

216
A creative use of mirrors: by covering the fireplace surround with a wide piece of mirror, the reflected light from a small window opposite it is amplified.

217
The mirror also acts as a glamorous frame for what would otherwise be a less dynamic mantel.

218
Tall candlesticks balance the horizontal composition of a mantelpiece and give the entire room height.

219
A simple raised hearth can serve as a seating ledge as well as a surface for displaying a few prized objects.

220
Turn a fireplace into the meditative focus of a serene room by limiting furniture to one or two pieces.

221

Keep it simple—an intricately carved

mantelpiece is a work of art in itself

and needs very little else in the way of

adornment.

A fireplace is a pivotal feature in a room—but what separates the predictable from the innovative?

223
Use a decorative fabric on a Chinese vase screen to place in front of the fireplace in the off-season. This attractive screen can be used to accent another area when it's time to fire up.

224
Log storage may take a casual form such as free-standing shelves stacked with bins of kindling. This method merges the old timber with the room's post-and-beam construction.

225
Whimsical screens that refuse to take themselves too seriously add a note of surprise and delight to their surroundings.

226
To avoid the look of a big black hole in the middle of the room, the walls around a large plain fireplace can be mirrored. This doubles the room's size and balances the flameless fireplace's impact.

How to Build the Best Fire

227
Begin with a layer of crumpled newspaper, then crisscross kindling on top.

228
For the fire to receive oxygen, the newspaper and the kindling need to be loose enough for air to circulate.

229
Add three logs on top. Open the damper completely, make a torch of rolled newspaper, and wave the burning torch under the damper to heat the chimney air. The lighted torch can be used to ignite the bed of newspaper.

230
A periodic cleaning and inspection of the fireplace is a necessary part of maintenance, as is the installation of a chimney cap to prevent animals from nesting in the flue.

Symmetry and Balance

231
The cohesiveness of composition depends on the relationships of various elements in a room. Both contrast and harmony are two valid approaches.

232
An example of contrast is a severe, straight chair juxtaposed with an over-stuffed and cozy sofa.

233
Asymmetry is interesting as well—three photos on one side of a mantel with a single vase on the other side—or nothing at all. Balance is achieved between open and closed spaces—textures in a room can mimic those elements outside its windows. Garden ornaments poised on a pedestal reflect the garden beyond.

Striking a balance in decorating and design is a very important concept. For every design action, there is an equal and opposite reaction.

Spatial equilibrium is as important as matching fabrics. Evidence candlesticks placed at either end of a table with a bowl of flowers in between, or two chairs flanking a sofa.

Harmony is achieved when colors, patterns,

and textures create a soothing design.

Walls, Windows & Floors

Walls, windows, and floors are physical elements in a room. The way they are treated—or not—relays messages about you and the room. If walls are busy with patterns they will give off an exuberant feeling; floors luxuriously carpeted relay a sense of comfort; and windows facing out on a garden may be treated minimally, with no curtains or shades at all—all of these are basic choices that determine how the character of a room is formed.

Each of these elements relies on the others for unity and must be compatible in color, texture, and scale. If any one of these basics is not harmonious, new features can be introduced. A new stair railing may be installed or a distinctive molding might be added. What is important to keep in mind is that things can always be altered. The treatments then depend on how subtle or elaborate you want to be.

The Ultimate Tips for Hanging

237 When you take pictures to a framer, bring snapshots of your rooms. They will help you determine the appropriate frames.

238 Select a sturdy hammer, and don't choke the neck. If you hold it lower, the nail will go in more smoothly.

239 Buy a contractor-quality metal measuring tape. Cloth ones are too flimsy and don't lie flat on walls.

240 Use a pencil to make markings—ballpoint pens leave indelible marks.

241 A level is a must for placing frames, mirrors, and brackets. Your ladder should have an attached surface or tray for holding tools. Hang with a friend: you'll need an extra pair of hands and eyes.

242 Consider the room's purpose. You will want to see your living room's pictures from a seated position; if you're straining your neck to look at them, they are too high. In a hallway, where you are always standing, hang pictures higher.

243 Mirrors look smashing over a fireplace if you hang them low enough to see yourself—it also makes ceilings appear higher.

244 Never hang mirrors less than two feet above a sofa—or you will see the back of everyone's head all evening.

245 *Near smaller fireplaces, sconces should be about eight inches from the sides of the opening.*

246

Arrange small-

to medium-size

frames in

friendly groups

with no more

than six inches

of wall between

any two pictures.

Do not hang

anything near

doors.

247 Do not hang pictures any lower then ten inches above the top of the sofa. Guests' gesturing arms and hands grasping glasses should not come into contact with your prized possessions.

248 When hanging sconces near a fireplace, consider the mantel width. In general, sconces should be placed 68 inches from the floor to the electrical box. If your fireplace is very wide, they should be hung over both ends of the mantel, not way off to the side or too close together.

249 As for dining room lanterns or chandeliers, always place them over the center of the table. From the tabletop to the bottom of the fixture, there should be 30 to 36 inches—no lower. For those who move their dining tables around to make room for buffets and more guests, use an S-hook on the chain to lift the fixture up five or six notches to accommodate people walking under it.

If you hang brackets over your bed, you will definitely want to Fun-Tak or hot-glue the vases, pots, urns, or ginger jars you display on top of them.

Hanging plates and platters only makes sense in rooms where you might be dining. More is best. Your plate display doesn't have to match, but there should be some continuity of theme. Hang your collection above a focal point—a fireplace, buffet, or large console. A plate collection mounted on a dining room screen adds an interesting dimension.

If you want to install swing-arm lamps by your bed, they should be anchored 42 inches above the floor and about eight inches away from the headboard—higher beds might require a slight increase to these measurements.

Wallpaper Tips

253

Most wallpaper is sold in double and triple rolls to ensure that all the paper used for a job is from the same dye lot—it is priced by the roll.

254

Pattern and run numbers are printed on each roll during manufacturing. These numbers identify papers from the same "run," or batch. Because different dye lots produce slight variations in color and texture, it's important that all rolls designated for a particular project are from the same run.

255

Your walls contain more square footage than any other decorative surface in a room. Adding a distinctive wallcovering is the quickest and most affordable way to define the overall character and feel of a space.

To determine how much you will need, begin by measuring wall height from floor to ceiling, excluding baseboards and moldings. Next measure the length of each wall including doors and windows. Find your total square footage by multiplying ceiling height by wall length and divide that number by the square feet in the roll of wallpaper you plan to use. Most rolls contain between 25 and 30 sq. ft. of wallpaper per single roll.

Things to consider when choosing wallpaper include the type of room you're papering and your family's lifestyle. Then look for attributes that fit your needs. Some common paper types include scrubbable papers designed to withstand mildly abrasive brushes and detergents; washable papers that may be sponged clean to remove fingerprints and grime; and colorfast wall-coverings that resist fading when exposed to sunlight. Strippable wallpapers are easily peeled from the wall, leaving behind a minimum of paste and residue. Prepasted papers have been treated with a water-activated adhesive, making them easier to hang.

You Can Do It Yourself!

258
Samples can be obtained from retailers who are willing to lend you sample books overnight. Mail-order and Internet sites generally make swatches available to you, though some companies do charge a small fee for samples. It's best not to purchase wallcovering without first looking at a sample of it in your own home, where lighting, furnishings, and other elements in the room may affect your decision.

259
Home improvement outlets, paint retailers, and design centers should have all the current sample books from a variety of manufacturers. For comparison shopping, also consider wallpaper Web sites and mail-order companies that specialize in wallcoverings.

260
Wallpaper removal: Most papers produced within the last 15 or so years are strippable, meaning that they should peel from your walls with little effort. However, if the paper is resistant to removal, you may have to do a little extra work. Start by scoring the wallcovering with a "paper tiger" tool available at hardware stores. Next, apply adhesive remover and allow it to soak through. Once dry, the paper should peel easily.

Wallpapering is a popular do-it-yourself

project and is relatively easy to learn.

The prices of the wall-coverings vary greatly. Standard printed papers start at $5.00 per roll and go up from there, depending on the complexity of the pattern and the type of paper used. If you've chosen a delicate, expensive paper for a room chock-full of nooks and crannies, you may want to go with a pro. Most wallcovering retailers will provide a list of skilled paperhangers in your area.

To prepare your wall for wallpapering, smooth out any rough spots and apply one coat of latex primer to the entire area you'll be papering. The primer provides a clean surface for best adherence and ensures easy stripping when it comes time to replace your wallcovering.

264

Choosing the right pattern for a room is a personal decision. Inspiration can come from anywhere. To help focus on your design preferences, start a folder of magazine clippings, color chips, fabric swatches, etc. You'll probably see certain styles or motifs repeated over and over.

265

Add architectural interest to flat walls by placing a wallpaper border 36 inches from the floor to create an instant chair rail. Install the same pattern 6 inches to 12 inches down from the ceiling to replicate crown molding. In the nursery, choose a neutral wallcovering and finish it off with a "baby" border. As your child grows, update the room by replacing the building blocks with baseballs or ballerinas without redoing the entire wall.

Consider the size of the room and any architectural features you want to highlight or hide. Design professionals often follow these simple guidelines: geometric patterns, including plaids and vertical stripes, draw the eye upward, making ceilings appear higher. Large prints make an oversized room appear smaller and more intimate. Small prints add visual interest and background color to open up cramped rooms or tiny spaces.

Picture Perfect: Choosing the Right Frame

267 It's important to distinguish between significant works of art and pictures—the prints, lithographs, drawings, black-and-white photographs that most of us can afford.

268 There should be some sort of dialogue between the frame and what's inside it, whether it echoes the work, or is in direct opposition.

269 Once you have decided on the frame, you must address the mats—size and color, double or French.

Paintings of merit are traditionally hung in

frames appropriate to the period in which

they were painted.

271 If the picture is vertical, increase the width to make the whole look more square. As a rule the bottom section of a mat is slightly deeper—about ¹/4 to ¹/2 inch—to counteract the optical illusion that makes the top seem heavier.

272 Use silk mats for formal, classic photographs, sometimes adding a bead of gold on the bevel (the inside edge) to imbue the print with a reflective quality.

273 Choose a thick 8-ply mat board rather than 4-ply. A deeper mat creates a window for the art, attracting the eye.

274 For black-and-white photographs, match the color of the mat to the paper the photo is printed on— photo white for new photographs and antique white for old ones.

275 *The best framers have an artist's eye and a craftsman's concern for quality.*

French mats, hand-colored with a series of wash lines, are a traditional treatment. Elegant for antique prints and watercolors, they are out of place in more contemporary pieces.

Never put a linen mat on an oil painting. This suggests that the painting is not good enough to stand on its own.

Conservation is a concern—mats should be made of rag board, as used in museums, and backings should be acid-free. If there is no mat, use fillets to separate the artwork from the glass to give it room to breathe and to prevent condensation.

Study molding samples in each shop, talk to the owner, and look at what is hanging on the frame-shop's walls.

A good framer will have a range of styles and prices, offering the best quality within each category.

The difference between a really good frame and a less expensive one is that you can see the joints in the latter because it is made of prefinished materials cut to size.

Ask a framer what else he or she has in the basement or back room. Frames that have been rejected or removed from other works are often less expensive and have more personality.

The most common mistake people make is hanging pictures too high. The old rule about putting them at standing eye level doesn't work because people are usually sitting. When in doubt, hang it three inches below what you think.

Don't color coordinate the mat and frame with the décor of a room. The location of a painting or print can and should change.

Movability is one reason designers prefer to prop pictures on ledges or suspend them from rails or hanging rods—when something is in one place for too long you stop looking at it.

In framing a collection, create continuity through color—all black or all gold leaf—but vary frame styles to avoid monotony.

Put detailed works in small frames in accessible locations; bolder compositions can be hung further away.

The best frame doesn't compete with the art for attention—it enhances without stealing the show.

When grouping pictures on a wall consider

the overall composition.   There should be a

consistent spacing factor between each picture.

How to Treat Your Windows

290 A valance hung on top of draw draperies lends wonderful drama. Take your valance up to the ceiling and make sure it is not more than one-third the height of the whole window treatment.

291 The visual interest of treatments are enhanced by decorative flourishes at the curtain and valance edges.

292 Make sure a curtain rod extends about 12 inches on either side past the French doors. This will make the doorway look wider.

It's nice when curtains hit the floor with a one-inch break. This is called puddling. If you do choose to puddle your draperies, make a statement and go all the way with at least a foot of extra fabric.

Don't assume that you have to use exactly the same window treatment on every window in a room.

If you use different types of treatments in one room, definitely use the same fabric for continuity.

To compensate for a room with little architectural interest, try using curtains with contrasting borders, tassels, appliqués, or beads.

In a modern house, keep it simple with scrims or shades that don't compete with the room's clean lines.

If your ceilings are low, hang your curtain rod higher than the window frame. This will make the panels longer and your room will feel bigger.

Most fabrics lend themselves to being used as draperies, unless they are extremely stiff or heavy. Textiles woven with materials such as hemp or sisal don't drape well; use them as window shades instead. Even corduroy can make great-looking curtains.

Use linings to prolong the life of your curtains. They act as a sunblock preventing any fabric, but especially costly ones, from fading prematurely.

Linings are a must with statelier fabrics—or when privacy is necessary. When curtains are pulled back the linings show, so use a sateen fabric.

"Simple curtains" are best made from gingham or batiste. You will get an airy and open feeling, but just be prepared to replace the curtains sooner.

Help insulate your rooms by using an interlining of cotton or wool flannel. The added weight will not only keep the cold out, but will also give the draperies a grander appearance.

Cut your costs—make great curtains out of inexpensive fabrics or sheets— as long as you put effort into the design, draping, and trim.

If you choose a big, bold stripe for your window treatment, keep the style a little conservative so it doesn't become overwhelming.

When hanging curtains over French doors you don't want a valance because it will get in the way of the doors.

Be careful when covering your shades with plaid. Unless the grid is completely square, it can make your shades look off-kilter.

Tie the colors of your window treatments to something else in the room. Don't use the same pattern on the window treatments that you've used on the furniture or the walls.

If you are blessed with a great view, keep window dressings to a bare minimum (or perhaps none at all). Clear vistas open up your house and make it feel as if it goes on forever.

Carpet Tip Primer

310

Physically measure the area before ordering carpet—don't rely on architectural plans.

311

Carpets come in limited widths and may need to be fitted together, so ask the installer for a seaming plan. A seam should go under a bed, for example, rather than through the middle of a room. Make note of patterns, ribs, or stripes and the direction they should run.

312

Vacuum at least once a week and have carpets professionally steam-cleaned annually.

Staircase carpets are the most difficult to install. Watch for "smiles," which occur when carpet is bent and shows its backing through piles or fibers.

314 Sprinkling salt on carpet an hour before vacuuming brightens it.

315 Treat stains immediately. Blot them with clean white towels or napkins—never rub or brush.

316 Sprinkle grease stains with cornmeal or baking soda, leave overnight, and vacuum in the morning.

317 For more tips check out www.carpet.org.

Melt ice cubes over indentations left by

furniture legs to restore the pile.

Ambience & Lighting

This chapter offers guidance for creating the right atmosphere through both practical and whimsical means. Careful attention to detail is required when placing objects, possessions, and even outlets in a room.

When it comes to lighting, ambience refers to the general illumination of interiors, their shapes, and dimensions. It is important to have the right light appropriately distributed so that rooms may be bathed in the proper glow—but never glare. When conceptualizing a lighting plan, you must remember that the source of light should be concealed. Lighting should never confront you, but should be beautifully orchestrated and hidden.

Lighting may also be thought of in terms of spheres and zones—this refers not only to actual lighting sources, but also to materials and techniques that set a mood in a room. Textures, scents, music, and even an alluring candy dish full of rich chocolates work magically toward building an certain aura and a feel in your home.

Your
Rooms
Will Look
and Feel
More
Romantic
if You . . .

Arrange full, low, rounded
bouquets of pink, orange,
and red roses.

Plant a terra-cotta pot with
white lilies.

Invest in deep down and
feather upholstery.

Animate a staircase or
bathroom with Zubor
pastoral mural.

Upholster an armchair in
red leather.

Flank a sofa with papier-
mâché side tables.

Trim silk lamp-shades with silk braid.

Stoke your fireplace with real crackling logs.

Choose a pair of exaggerated, curvy andirons.

Toss in a fluffy

mohair and

angora throw in

a soothing,

natural color.

Mix a pretty mirrored cabinet with statelier pieces.

Keep your stereo system out of sight.

Play Brazilian music in the background.

Favor intense purple or red and white toile prints.

Line all your lampshades in shell-pink silk.

Arrange a few branches of blood-red coral on your mantel.

Display peonies in almost any size, color, or configuration.

Trim your curtains with pretty, puffy pom-poms.

Place a large painted tole tray with a worn and faded look on your cocktail or sofa table.

Use luxurious leopard, cheetah, or tiger print to upholster a footstool or ottoman.

Buy an old rug with a florid pattern.

Select a clock that chimes out the hours.

Try a bench or a sofa with serious silk cord and tassel trim.

Frame your Flemish still lifes in a modern way.

Hide your TV set.

Use tailored silver candlesticks and long white tapers.

Consider a clock encased in real leather.

Add a pair of sofa pillows covered in crushed silk velvet.

Try single-layered, oyster-colored taffeta curtains in front of windows that are slightly ajar.

Hang a slightly oversized rock-crystal

teardrop chandelier.

349

Use a table

topper over a

tablecloth over

a table skirt:

layers!

Ironing bed

linens with

scented water

imparts a subtle

fragrance and a

hint of romance.

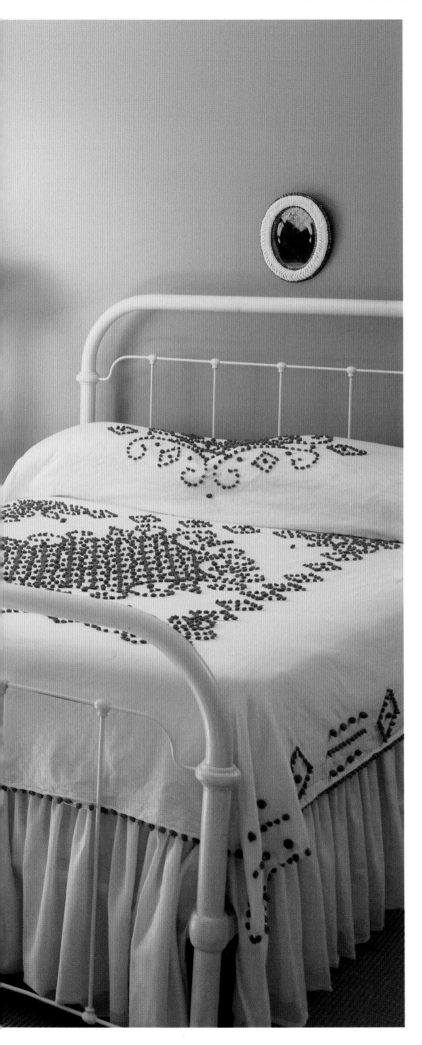

Display luscious candies in a

beautiful dish.

The Lowdown on Lighting

It is important to learn the terms before you begin:

Incandescent bulb: produces a yellowish-white light that is emitted in all directions; available either clear or frosted.

Fluorescent bulb: Uses $1/2$ to $1/3$ as much electricity as incandescent bulbs with comparable lumen ratings, and lasts up to 20 times longer. Available as slim tubes; screw-in types can be used in place of incandescents in standard lamp sockets. Available in a wide spectrum of colors; warm white tones best duplicate the color of incandescent bulbs.

Tungsten-halogen bulb: produces a bright, white light. Has longer life and provides more lumens per watt than regular incandescent bulbs. Available in both line voltage (120 volts) and low voltage (12 volts); low-voltage types require a transformer to step down the voltage.

The Larger the Room, the More Lighting.

356

Experts agree that it's better to allow about 2.5 to 3 watts of light per square foot of space. To calculate this figure, first multiply the room's width by its length. This equation provides the room's total square footage. Next, add up the wattages of every bulb in all the fixtures you intend to put in the room. (Be sure the wattages don't exceed the manufacturer's recommendations for each fixture.) Then, divide the total square footage by the total number of watts. The final number of watts is the measurement of watts of light per square foot. Keep in mind, though, that if the room is full of dark furniture or has dark walls, or if you plan to use dark lampshades, you might need to slightly exceed the 2.5- to 3-watt range. The same holds true if the room has a very high ceiling.

When creating

a lighting plan,

it's critically

important to

determine how

much overall

illumination each

room demands.

When building and remodeling a house you can maximize light and views—but simply adding lots of windows or window walls is not the best solution.

The interior architecture
of a house does include
windows.

Location, exposure and
privacy are all equally
important considerations.

Lighting a loft space can
be tricky. In true loft
spaces, very often the windows run only along one
wall. This creates lighting
and ventilation challenges.

Due to some unavoidable
limitations, lighting in lofts
is almost as critical as the
placement of windows.

The Pleasure Principle

How to make a room sensuous and lighter than air—easily!

363 You can brighten a room with your hardware. A faceted doorknob reflects the light, and glass knobs glint in a kitchen.

364 Veil a weathered wrought-iron garden table with ethereal organza.

365 While setting a mood you also must be practical—upholster a sofa in plain white canvas so you can spend more for something like a silk-flecked pillow with pearls.

366

To soften a room, arrange the light sources in a triangle. If you put lamps in all four corners, a room becomes static. And use frosted bulbs to cut the glare.

367 A room looks more organized when light switches and doorknobs are the same height, along with speaker volume controls and thermostats.

368 Try not to put a lamp in front of a window. At night the glass will turn into a mirror and you won't see out.

369 To get a designer look, use objects in a way they were never intended. Keep the paper towel roll in a low square glass vase. Sit soap in a wooden dish from a sushi bar.

370 Draping a round table always makes it look substantial, no matter how small. You don't even have to hem the material—tuck it under.

371 Unconstructed window treatments mean less sewing. For a simple yet dramatic curtain, drape white organza over a pole, then tie the front panel into a loose knot to create some shape.

372 To create a room within a room hang translucent parachute nylon from the ceiling; walls and doors would block the light. Nothing is more beautiful than to see fabric moving in the breeze. The buoyant nylon creates a sense of coolness.

373 If you're tired of a rug, turn it upside down for a new look.

374

Put your sofa in a spot with the most

natural light and you'll be happy.

Ways to Warm Up Your Room

375

Plop a crushed velvet pillow on every armchair.

376

Paint your old magazine rack Chinese red.

377

Cover your slipper chairs in something fuzzy.

378

Trim your curtains in scarlet passementerie.

Spruce up your

old fireplace tools.

Serve your red

wine in cut-

crystal decanters.

Freshen up your powder room with plain, crisp linen hand towels.

Find a better place for your foul weather gear.

Daylight is a bright time— but at night try just using candles.

Change your neutral terry-cloth bath mat for a colorful, fluffy one.

Stack six or seven juicy biographies on all bedside tables.

Cover your parchment lampshades with red plaid taffeta.

Light three scented candles in your entry hall.

Find a small tole tray for your mail and keys.

Dress up bathrooms with tiny silver vases filled with tiny pink roses.

Line your closet floors with toile de Jouy wallpaper.

Flank your fireplace with big baskets of pinecones.

Whip up some Kir cocktails for your next do.

Mix floral bouquets with sprigs of berries.

394

Pull two extra chairs up to your sofa.

395 Hand-print the place cards at your next dinner party.

396 Upholster a footstool in rich black paisley wool.

397 Sprinkle deep chocolate desserts with powdered sugar.

398 Serve light-colored food on dark china, and vice versa.

399 Arrange a flock of family photos on your mantel.

400 Play Baroque music during dinner.

Go with a deep shade of red on the floor.

402

Get a pair of larger andirons.

403

Hang a few jingle bells on your pooches' collar.

404

Spray your dressing room with a spicy scent.

405

Present a beef and wild mushroom stew on a terra cotta platter.

406

Place a huge silver bowl piled with Washington State Apples on your cocktail table.

107

Festoon your arched doorway with a leafy

autumnal garland.

Gussy up your

porch with a

pair of conifer

topiaries.

Back your sofa

with a long, high

console table.

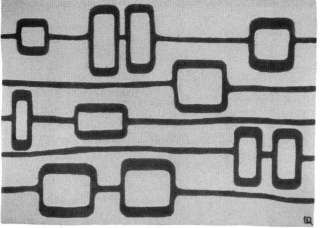

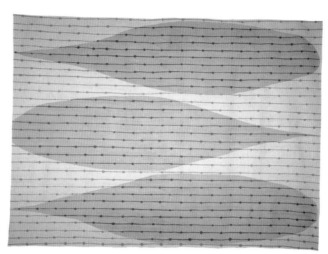

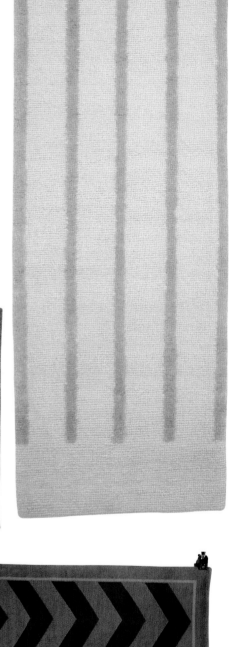

410

Cover your carpet with a few exotic area rugs.

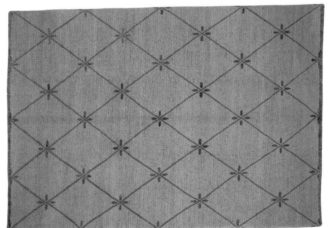

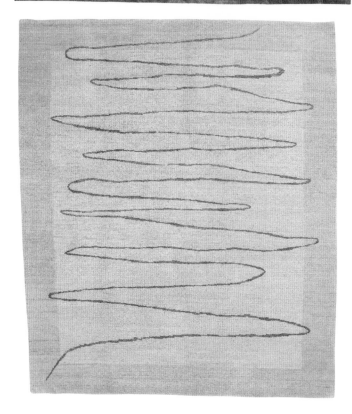

411 Sheath your orchid in a wicker basket.

412 Pair every armchair with a really good reading lamp.

413 Trash old ashtrays.

414 Exchange 100-watt bulbs for 75s.

415 Buy a set of cream soup spoons and use them.

416 Install dimmers on every light in the house.

417 Lower your dining room chandelier eight inches.

418 Enliven your entryway with a cheery umbrella stand.

419

Banish fluorescent lighting from the kitchen.

420

Cozy up occasional tables with votives and mini bowls of treats.

421

Serve hot toddies in tumblers.

422

Repaint your front door.

428

Mix materials in your table settings.

Personalize & Accessorize

A single piece of furniture can symbolize privacy. A dressing table, wing chairs, or chaise has the capability to make such an individual statement. Designed to be autonomous, a writing desk or chest can mark a quintessential private spot. The placement of a silver box, candlestick, or leather photo album can speak worlds about the private mark one wants to make in a room.

Dressing an individual and dressing a room have much in common when it comes to making a personal statement. Fabric is an incredible tool for conveying distinctive and unique qualities. Rich velvet, striped silk, lustrous taffeta, and anything leopard print—each makes a statement. Distinctive prints and soft chenille delight the eye and whisk the beholder away to a faraway land or draws him or her into a tactile experience. Flowers, perfume, wind chimes, and charcoal sketches scintillate the senses and leave you, and others, with your very intimate signature.

Command-ments of Decorating

The space you leave

empty is as important

as the space you fill.

Minimalism is always at war with real life.

Interiors are shapes in
space. Size really does
matter. Scale and propor-
tion are everything.

It doesn't matter whether
something is antique or
not. What counts is
presence, not provenance.

Chanel said you should
get all dressed up with
your jewelry on, then look
in the mirror and take one
thing off. Design is a comparable editing process.

Nothing is too humble to be dismissed—from winding laundry twine around chair legs, making curtains out of gold metal coffee-filter mesh to a perfectly crumpled brown-paper-bag-inspired lampshade!

Some designers feel that matching is a trademark of an amateur—others disagree—in the end it is your personal preference that matters.

Contemporary doesn't mean stark.

Use all the space in a room. Pull a sofa out from a wall and put a covered table behind it, providing a place for a reading lamp and accessories (plus Christmas ornaments, wallpaper rolls, and bolts of fabric, all stored underneath).

An object by itself is only an object.

Juxtapose it with something else and it

becomes a composition.

434

Follow the archi-

tecture—find

what you can

use from the

architecture and

then go with it or

against it.

Great Tips on Accessorizing:

A great painting

or a giant mirror

makes a true

mark in a room.

436 Behind a sofa, hang a large painting flanked by smaller ones.

437 Accessories should always seem personal, not store-bought. They should tell a story.

While accessories give a room character, don't over-do it.

Don't spread accessories around evenly. Group them to make a point.

Cleanliness is next to god-liness.

On a mantel, place a handsome clock flanked by a pair of cachepots. Also try tea boxes and a single candlestick.

On the side tables keep it simple: a lamp, a saucer, a box or a small sculpture.

Walls of books are the best decoration of all. You can never have too many of them.

Big floor pillows make for fun room accessories.

If you are using flora inside, go with real flowers or dried hydrangeas for a permanent arrangement.

446 Candles are always romantic, but be careful about where you place the strong-scented ones.

447 Side tables can be even simpler: just a telephone, or nothing, so that you can put down a drink.

448 Found objects are beautiful on a mantel: an interesting stone or piece of driftwood, or a colorful child's sculpture.

Symmetry helps anchor a room, but should not be the rule. Try asymmetrical arrangements.

450

Perch a painting atop a mirror—these

surprising juxtapositions add endless character

to a simple room.

Display only

things that you

love and that

have meaning.

Ways to Personalize Your Rooms

Line up candle-sticks on your fireplace mantel.

Honor favorite family photos with good-quality frames.

454 Add a contrasting color trim to your living room curtains.

455 Flank every comfortable chair with a magazine rack or stand.

456 Toss one-of-a-kind throws over the arms of sofas and wing chairs.

457 Frame every piece of art differently.

458 Fill shallow wooden boxes or small deep trays with colored pencils so that you can sketch or make lists whenever the urge arises.

459 Position a footstool in front of your favorite armchair.

460 Throw a colorful area rug on top of your sisal carpet.

461 Use two different sizes of pink or red roses for bouquets.

462 *Stand small-framed watercolors on side tables.*

Go easy on symmetry—more than three

matched pairs of anything in a single room is

too much.

Accessorize a large sofa with a dozen smallish pillows in six different prints.

Group family photos on one large sofa table.

466

Unmatch your

table lamps.

Take advantage of a tall
cabinet: fill it to the gills
with your treasures.

Accent accessories with
braid or grosgrain ribbon.

Slide a child-size chair to
the side of your fireplace.

Stack books and magazines
on chairs and bedside tables.

Buy a bigger, prettier
umbrella stand.

Cover the top of a wooden
sideboard with a pretty
linen cloth.

Reframe your photos
and works on paper in
different-colored mattings.

Place mini CD players on
bedside tables in guest
rooms.

Hang your favorite pic-
tures on the most promi-
nent wall.

Buy a new pet bed for
your dog or cat and cover
it in a perky toile or
provençal print.

Stack books and magazines on chairs and bed-side tables.

478 Add berries to your flower arrangements.

479 Five minutes before guests arrive, spray your favorite perfume in the foyer.

480 For holiday dinners, give every guest a hand-picked party favor.

481 Upholster a bedroom chair in crewelwork fabric.

482 Dress up your four-poster bed with a sheer canopy of pale gauzy cotton.

483 Use an underskirt and a topper for your dining room table.

Paint one wall in your living room a contrasting color.

Contrast your

tablecloth and

napkin colors.

Lean diminutive

paintings against

a stack of books.

Have your good sheets and towels

monogrammed.

488

Invest in an

array of bed

throws and

change them

every month.

Flowers, Flowers, Flowers

489 Even before unwrapping your flowers, prepare a clean vase with fresh cold water. Refill the vase every day.

490 Using a sharp knife, cut the stems on the diagonal, one flower at a time. Garden roses don't absorb water easily, so make a clean, long-angled cut.

491 Flowers should be in vases, not only on fabrics.

Stock your bar with glasses in myriad shapes.

Store your mascara, eye pencils, and lipsticks in a battery of silver-plated cups.

494

Use different patterns of china for

every course.

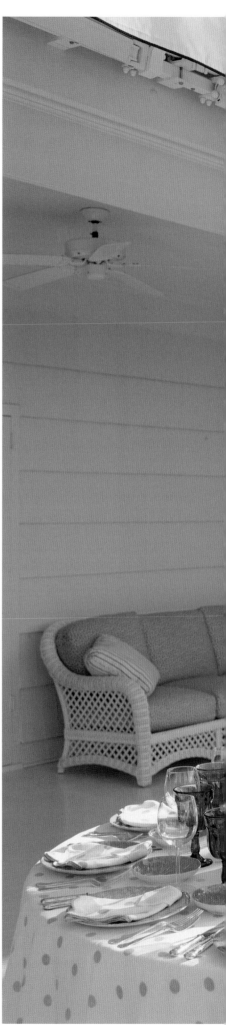

495 Hand-embroider your guest towels.

496 Design a "centerpiece scene" of small to medium bouquets rather than one large one.

497 Serve drinks on large and small trays lined with crisp linen napkins.

498 Sheathe your houseplants in friendly old toled cachepots.

499 Play the piano for friends.

500 Recite a poem at your next dinner party.

501 An antique linen sheet over a round dining room table relieves a room of heaviness and makes it much more personal and softer.

Taking Care of Linens & Silver

502

When it comes to sheets, don't be fooled by thread count. A 200 count where it's one thread is better than something higher where it's two over two.

503

Pillows—100 percent white Polish down recommended—can and should go into the washing machine, to get rid of the body oils that leave stains. Wash them alone, once with soap, twice without.

504

Never put fabric softener in with the towels. It ruins the absorbency.

Try lavender water in the steam iron, especially for guest room linens.

Keep your kitchen silver out. Silver hidden away in felt bags is less likely to be used and enjoyed. Moreover, if it's in sight, you'll remember to clean it.

Twinkle® silver polish is recommended. Polish whatever piece or two catches your eye as part of the clean-up after a meal. This keeps the task from becoming overwhelming.

Silverplate that has become worn or pitted can be replated. Take it to a local plating company.

Expert Tips for Storing and Preserving Heirlooms and Vintage Treasures at Home

509
Protect textiles from light, heat, humidity extremes, dust, pollution, and pests.

510
Avoid mothballs and dry cleaning bags, attics, basements, and closets next to pipes that might leak.

511
Textiles should never touch wood or cardboard, which cause chemical interactions.

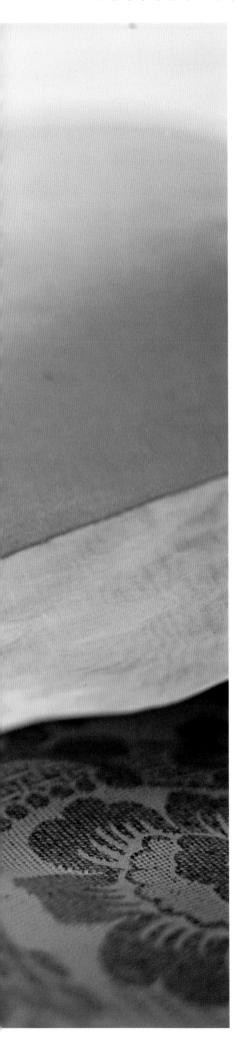

Sturdy quilts and textiles can be folded, but be sure to pad the folds with tissue and refold periodically to avoid creases.

For small pieces—samplers, embroideries—investigate metal archival flat files, finished in powder-coated paint.

Always line your boxes with neutral pH-tissue, a well-washed cotton sheet, or muslin that's unbleached and desized.

When stacking textiles, layer them with archival tissue to protect one item from another.

Seasonal Decorating

Adjust the feel of your home to the changing seasons.

Create seasonal still lifes of fruit and flowers. Based on what's fresh at the market, introduce different colors into a room. Then add a complementary tablecloth, cushions and paintings.

Nudge furniture away from fireplaces in the summer—move it near them in the winter.

Take a sketchbook of watercolors, pose it on a mantel piece, and open the book to a different page at a whim.

The earth

goes through

constant cycles

of renewal—

your house

can, too.

520
Deploy Polaroids and Old Master postcards as spontaneous artwork.

521
Vary the look of a footstool by tying on a piece of linen with corner knots.

522
Instead of a curtain rod, string up a laundry line that allows the quick draping of a length of fabric.

523
Slip a seasonally-appropriate fabric over a chair, knotting it in the back to create a ball gown train.

Space & Storage

Storage is rarely abundant. Space, depending upon where you live, is even less so. Successfully wrestling with these problems often requires coming up with more than one solution. There are myriad ways to make the most of whatever you have. You can play with paint or paintings to give a small room the expanse of a larger one; a major piece of furniture can work in the tiniest of rooms; or a wall unit that stores books and CDs can also serve as a room divider. One thing everyone must remember is that the size of a room is as much a matter of perception as it is of square footage. Pattern and color can work magic in creating an illusion of roominess. Small is bigger, and big becomes bigger when each is juxtaposed to the other.

Storage is both about hiding things as well as showing them off. Decisions should be based on what you have, where you use it, and where you want it kept. The following tips can make your home not only more visually attractive, but more practical and livable.

Drama on a Small Stage:

Dealing with spatial constraint and a tight budget.

524 An ebony stain on wood floors "grounds" everything in the room and provides a substantial palette and strong point of focus.

525 A cost effective, space-stretching illusion is velvet-edged painter's cloth curtains hung wall-to-wall and floor-to-ceiling.

526 Find an inventive light fixture to draw the eye upwards in a small space.

A clever junk-

store salvage is

this cut-down

console uphol-

stered with

cream leather for

a coffee table.

A deep chocolate brown wall contrasting starkly with the furniture gives the illusion of a larger space.

Less is Best

One sure way to give a room a new look is to drastically reduce its contents. Decide what goes out and where to get rid of the castoffs!

First commandment: If you haven't sat in it, turned it on, or dumped the mail on it for three days, consider getting it out of the room.

Let in "fresh air:" When trying to decide what to get rid of, move furniture around and then automatically cart off at least fifteen percent.

Consider the proportions of the pieces in a room: something may be too delicate or too chunky. Whatever the misfit, admit it isn't right for the room, then toss it.

Remove small pieces that clutter a space such as undersize bedside tables. If it can't hold books, water, glasses, and an alarm clock then it's not doing its job.

If you sweep all your small pieces into a drawer and permit only one piece to return at a time, it's like discovering that object all over again.

Let sentiment prevail: a room should swing around your favorite things—imagine that you can only save three pieces from a room and clear out the rest of the clutter.

Everything you get rid of can be sold. Don't throw items away before offering them for sale.

For valuable pieces, first get an appraisal.

The more you research the antique or collectible— as well as who might want to buy it—the higher the price you will get.

Store dining chairs you don't

regularly use. (You can always bring them

back for a dinner party.)

540 Auction houses provide free estimates for items they might handle, and will often come to your house to do it.

541 Once you have a ballpark figure, decide whether to offer your piece to a consignment shop (usually for a 30 percent commission), sell it at an auction gallery (often for a 15 percent commission), or pay a small fee to advertise in appropriate publications or on the Internet (i.e.,www.ebay.com).

542 If you can't do the maintenance then put it away—picture frames, silver doodads, carved onyx, porcelain figurines—should never get tarnished, dull, or dusty.

Organize Every Room in Your House

To accommodate the ever-growing piles of books and magazines, you don't necessarily need to install more bookshelves. Simply stack them up under cocktail tables, sofa tables, and consoles. The piles should be neat, grouped by size, and lined up so that the spines face the same direction.

If your walls are full and you must show off a new print or watercolor, lean it against a fireplace mantel (summer only), in front of a large hanging mirror, or on the seat of a little-used side chair (this is not a childproof solution!).

China, napkins, tablecloths, crystal, glass, salt and pepper shakers, and silverware should be housed in dust- and grime-free cabinets or hutches.

Hang rarely used, attractive serving platters on walls.

Too many lampshades make a room look scattered and unfocused. Edit.

Devote one wide drawer to candles.

Keep throw pillows to a minimum, and never place them on small benches or seats.

If possible, store centerpiece vases and pots in the dining room for easy access.

When using your dining table for other projects, park your chairs at equal intervals around the walls.

Fabric- or leather-covered storage boxes with grosgrain or velvet ribbon ties will doll up your bedroom in a flash.

Buy a bed that's at least 11 inches off the floor and store luggage, off-season clothes, or even a bike underneath. Buy a long tailored skirt to hide it all.

Put extra buttons, collar stays, change, keys, business cards, etc., in silver, leather, or fabric-covered bowls and boxes.

Store infrequently used pots and bowls on the highest shelves in your kitchen.

Invest in airtight storage containers that are either clear or clearly marked.

You can unhook pots and pans from an overhead rack much more easily than you can dig them out of a noisy pile of metal in a dark cupboard.

Hang cooking utensils on your kitchen wall.

Store accessories behind a skirted bathroom sink.

Instead of many towel bars, install multilevel towel shelves high over the end of your bathtub.

A see-through shower curtain makes a small bathroom appear larger.

Glass-front cabinets and open shelving in the kitchen let you see everything at once.

Use a clever ladder-type structure for

pot-stacking.

Organizing
Your Closet

564
Measure your clothes on
their hangers before
installing rods. Double-
hang them above skirts
and pants.

565
Avoid using six different
kinds of hanger—wood is
best—and make sure they
all face the same way.

566
Hang skirts with skirts,
jackets with jackets.
Organize clothes by color.

567
Fold and stack sweaters
by color.

Don't pile things on the floor; if you keep it clear the carpet will be more spacious.

569
Display your pretty hand-
bags. If you can't see it
you won't use it.

570
Put a carpet or sisal on
the closet floor for a fresh
feeling.

571
Install a mirror on the
inside of the door.

572
Using an exposed light
bulb risks fire; choose a
covered fixture—and
make sure it's bright
enough.

573
Don't hold on to clothes
you haven't worn in a
year. It's easier to part with
old favorites if you donate
them to an organization.

574

Arrange shoes on shelves with heel out—it will help you decide which pair to wear.

Tiny Spaces, Huge Solutions

Make it look bigger...

575

Hang curtains up high, where the walls meet the ceiling.

576

Enlarge your small fireplace surround: make it taller and wider, not deeper.

577

Cover the floor with one large rug.

578

Lucite or glass cocktail and end tables are unobtrusive.

579

Install plain mirrored sconces on each side of your daybed.

Go for tailored,

neatly pleated

solid curtains or

crisp Roman

shades.

Select a tautly upholstered, streamlined, solid-colored sofa.

Use two standing lamps in the living room.

Place a mirrored screen in a corner.

Remove moldings, chair rails, and baseboards if your ceilings are low.

Choose textured fabrics rather than prints.

Build a floor-to-ceiling bookcase to cover one entire wall.

Light two off-white candles in two strategically placed silver candlesticks.

A checkered floor painted on the diagonal is a great space-swelling strategy.

In a tiny bedroom, when there is room for nothing else, all the character must come from the bed. A queen-size iron bed becomes the focal point by placing it at an angle.

590

Hide everything in plain sight! When faced with a tiny apartment space, try covering everything with the same pattern and it will seem to disappear.

591

The camouflage principle also works by papering the walls and upholstering the furniture with similar prints—flowers drop off the walls and onto the fabric!

592

Turn an unused kitchen corner into shallow storage. These 4^1/$_2$-inch shelves let the attractive contents show—while doors hide the less attractive things.

593

In a tiny apartment, books that would normally fill banished bookcases cleverly march up the stairs to the sleeping loft.

594

Hanging fabric panels can transform awkward rectangular rooms into more gracious square shapes and hide storage areas at the same time.

595

Stick with simple,

plain solid

lampshades.

Make it look cozier . . .

Tent the ceiling with a colorful pleated fabric.

Go for paisleys, Indian florals, crewelwork, embroidery, English chintzes, and wavy stripes.

Hang a wide, squat chandelier or a bowl-shaped fixture in the middle of the ceiling.

Accessorize armchairs and sofas with a dozen different patterned pillows.

Try two-seater sofas upholstered in compatible prints.

Find a florid, densely colored Oriental rug.

Use jewel-toned colors for lampshades. Place a half-dozen little side tables near armchairs and sofas.

Hang lots of photos, paintings, china, and brackets on the walls.

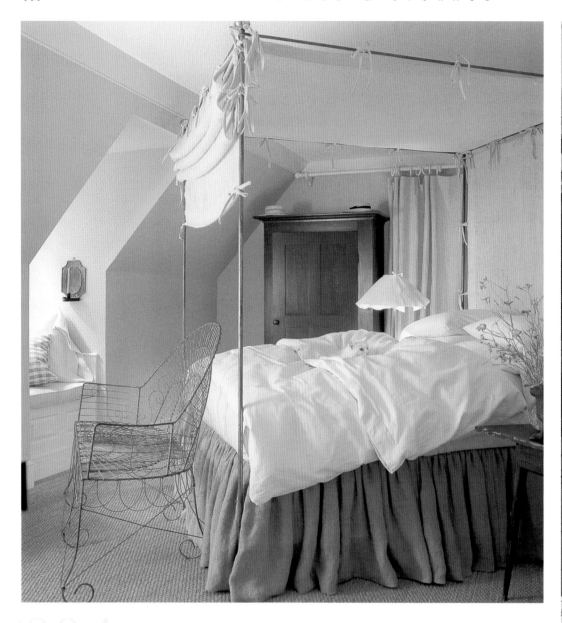

A room becomes unhinged and loses its sense

of boundary as soon as the floor, walls, and

ceiling no longer meet in well-defined corners.

Choose tones of pomegranate, coral, and

cinnabar for your walls or upholstery.

Where to Stash Your Stuff—Create a Clever Storage Unit

606 Choose fabrics with lots of character to make slipcovers for the shelves and add an amusing trim or valance to create the perfect witty hideaway.

607 Make the pattern by measuring the frame, adding an extra half inch for seam allowance, and laying out the pattern pieces on the fabric to factor in scale and repeat.

608 Figure out how the design will fall on the front so it can be divided to create two door panels.

609 The whole pattern is six pieces: top, back, two sides, and two door panels. If you add a valance, you need to create an additional pattern.

610 Use Velcro tabs to close the doors down the center and two one-way dressmaker zippers at the top to allow access to the interior.

611 *Start with industrial storage shelves on wheels. Use eye-catching fabrics to transform these units into stylish movable closets.*

612 For mobility and looks the wheels should remain unencumbered. But for safety's sake they should be locked.

613 Use your eye to fit the fabric to the frame. Where does the design fall, and do the motifs match and line up? Remember: measure twice, cut once.

614 These closets push the design envelope. Be creative, but don't go overboard. Use trims carefully; restraint keeps the unit chic.

615 To save on costs, use an inexpensive solid fabric for the closet's back panel, which will be hidden if it sits against a wall.

616 For easy access to the interior, keep valances no more than eight inches deep.

617 Grosgrain ribbon trim adds contrast and definition.

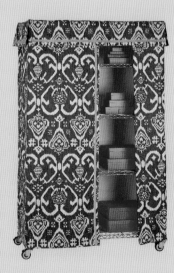

Find places for as many books as possible.

Use a combination of floor lamps, table lamps and picture lights.

Overdo it on the candles.

Order curtains that look like ball gowns—puffy taffeta that grazes the floor.

Decorating has never been more family friendly than it is today. If you have a family, no matter what age the children, you want your home to be livable and loved by all its occupants. Your home is the center for family life, and in being so it must be functional. This doesn't mean that your home can't be beautiful, stylish, and serve everyone's needs all at once.

This chapter helps you make choices about a whole host of issues as you decorate, renovate, maintain, nurture, and try to economize in this ever-changing environment for your family. Creating a safe home for you and your children is imperative. The child proofing tips that follow are very helpful, but are in no way all-inclusive. Please use our ideas and supplement with more detailed child proofing advice. Decorating can be costly so make your choices with an eye toward colors, fabrics, and furniture that can evolve as the family grows. Don't choose colors and upholstery that stand no chance against fingerprints and smudges. Select materials that clean up easily and are appropriate for raising happy children. Space and storage problems are bound to arise—here are some innovative and tasteful solutions for keeping clutter to a minimum.

Family-Friendly Decorating Tips

622
Avoid square corners on glass tabletops. Go curvy, and keep the cold glass-and-metal surfaces to a minimum.

623
Love seats and two-seater sofas are too small for family life—a long, deep sofa is best.

624
If you are tight on space, try retiring one of your armchairs or occasional chairs to make room for a second sofa.

625
If you have casters on the legs of your armchairs, make sure they lock.

626 Kids love beds that have some adventure to them: a sleigh bed—or any bed with a headboard and a footboard—feels cozy and safe. And it's much more fun for sleepovers.

627 Trying to preserve delicate fabrics in an active house is difficult. Pass on shiny solid satins, pale tone-on-tone damsks, plain cashmeres, and neutral solid linens.

Tile, stone, and concrete floors are hard, cold, and can be unpleasant for children without an area rug.

Tape electrical cords out of harm's way: under tabletops and down table legs. Use duct tape in colors that coordinate with your furniture.

Vases of flowers on low coffee tables will have to wait until your children can "look but don't touch."

Big potted plants also tempt kids to find the roots and dig in the dirt— try to avoid them.

If you can't manage to keep the toys out of the living room, invest in a big decorative wood or metal trunk/bin that you can place near the fireplace or under a table. You can even use it as a makeshift table if you slip a large antique tole tray on top.

For upholstery and wallpaper, choose motifs on tan, olive, caramel, brown or coral grounds. Fingerprints and smudges will be greatly reduced.

Great Kid-Friendly Rooms

634

Don't make a baby's room too juvenile.

635

Tired of blue? Try black, white, and fire engine red together.

636

Use blackout shades on the windows to encourage deep slumber.

637

Furnishings should grow with your child, so don't waste money on a changing table. Get a good-quality antique dresser and put a pad across the top.

Tired of just pink? Use colors like lilacs, and

apple green or reds.

639 Stick with patterned floor coverings or dark carpets that can handle spills. Choose broadloom, not modular tiles, since the latter's edges tend to lift up. A polyethylene film backing prevents paint and magic marker stains from soaking through to the padding underneath. Introduce a more interesting rug when the child is nine or so.

640 Hang artwork and posters on cork to avoid damaging the walls. You can also cover the corkboard with fabric.

641 Hang antique quilts and framed photocopies of kids' favorite illustrations.

642 If children are sharing the room, put beds on opposite sides of the room, creating a play space in between. Trundles are also ideal.

643 Don't skimp when buying a good mattress or a good carpet.

A baby is not a doll. A little extra space in

his or her room is priceless.

It is time to redecorate a child's room when functions change: crib to bed, LEGOs to computer. Otherwise, buy new bed sheets and bed spreads to give children a change.

Limit cutesiness to items that are easily replaced, like towels and rugs.

Children are rough on fabrics so don't invest in costly, delicate textiles. Use slipcovers made of machine-washable materials.

Opt for eggshell, satin, or semi-gloss finishes rather than flat paint, which is susceptible to scuff marks and scratches.

Avoid trendy decorating schemes. Cartoon-character fixations are quickly outgrown.

Light fixtures flush with the ceiling and sconces are best; avoid wiring.

Floral prints grow with your children.

Advice on the Maintenance Front

Think carefully before leaping into design decisions that could become maintenance nightmares.

Everyone has a different standard of perfection and tolerance for upkeep, so analyze your habits to avoid becoming a slave to cleaning.

Dark carpeting shows every speck of lint; Oriental rugs hide a multitude of sins.

Control clutter with lots of big open baskets for stacking newspapers, auction and gardening catalogs.

Absolutely the most practical upholstery fabric is beige or brown linen velvet.

Be realistic. If you can't keep dogs off your sofas, buy inexpensive washable cotton Indian bedspreads to tuck around the cushions.

Lined and interlined curtains will last from ten to twenty years and should never be dry-cleaned. To get rid of dust, lightly vacuum from behind.

Always use a fabric finish like Fiberseal for fragile silks, velvets, or suedes. The Pro-Tection brand comes with a stain kit and if that doesn't work, one of their experts will arrive to help.

Kitchen countertops made of solid surface synthetics such as Avonite or Corian are easiest to maintain—a scorch mark or scratch can be sanded out.

Gravel driveways may look great, but bits of stone stick to shoes, causing the ruin of many a marble or wood foyer floor.

The Agony & Ecstasy of Renovation

662 Determine need. Do you desire more space, or a better use of existing space? Are things getting a bit dog-eared, or do you need a visual lift? Have your tastes changed or evolved?

663 Make a wish list. Let your imagination run wild. (Reality checks will come in step 3.) Create a dream file by clipping pictures of appealing rooms, wall colors, carpets, lighting, furniture, and fabrics from interior design magazines. Eventually a theme will emerge, such as a color scheme or architectural style.

664 Establish a budget. Determine what you can spend then slash it by 20 percent, which you can put aside as a contingency fund for the inevitable snag. (If you do meet your budget, that 20 percent will enable you to buy that extra-special something.)

665 After establishing a budget, create a folder for each room and add pictures of existing furniture (and furniture to be bought), lighting possibilities, architectural detailing, fabric swatches and trims, wallpaper samples, and paint chips. Take them out of the folder when the budget dictates.

666 Visualize the project further by sketching "storyboards" depicting the room plan, with the furniture and decorating details in place. Use the storyboards as a two-dimensional dollhouse moving elements around until you arrive at what you want the finished project to look like. You will save time and avoid costly mistakes.

667 Make several photocopies of each room's floor plan and use them as a canvas to plot out the interior.

668 Learn to use an architect's scale ruler to draw furniture and read floor plans.

669 Create files for the following: moldings, millwork, cornices, and windows and door casements; windows and doors; kitchen and bath hardware and fixtures; electrical outlet plates and light switches; lampshade shapes and finishes (include measurements); paint chips, glazes, finishing techniques, and floor stains.

Headboards should be wood, leather, or slip covered for those mornings when everyone piles into bed.

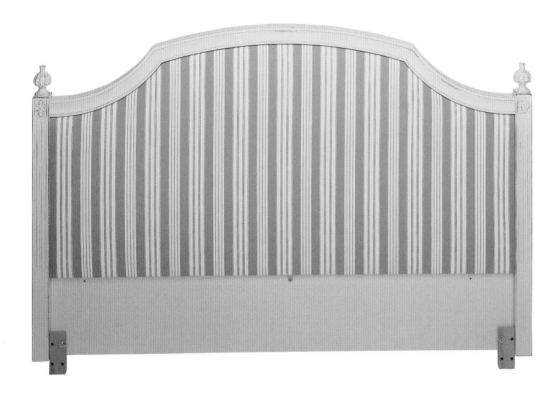

If you have animals, avoid glamorous silk curtains that puddle and provide a place for dog and catnapping. High swags and jadots or tailored Roman shades will remain hair-free.

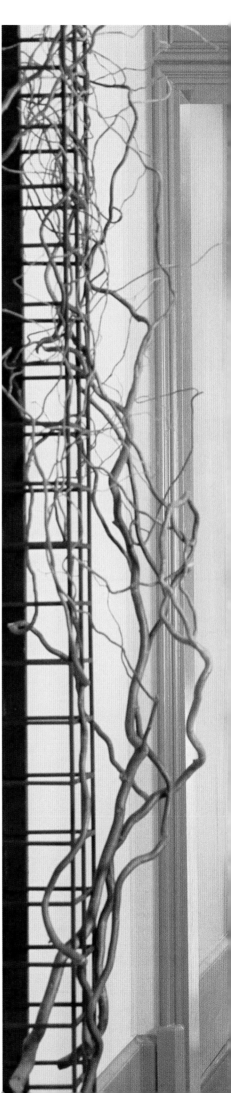

672 Grout sealers are not perfect. If you feel compelled to go at it with a toothbrush, then tile countertops are not for you.

673 For kitchen floors, forget white unless it has some kind of pattern or texture.

674 For families with children: no wall-to-wall carpeting; choose satin finish paint, not flat, for walls; no sharp-cornered glass-and-steel coffee tables—washable aniline-dyed leather-upholstered ottomans cushion the fall.

675 Always prewash fabric for slipcovers, and order two sets.

Antique case pieces are a good choice, since

any scratches only enhance their patina.

Conversely, pull-up chairs should be modern

so they don't creak or break.

Planning a Landscape that Helps Save on Energy Costs

677 In cold climates, try to decrease the impact of the wind and capture the greatest amount of heat from the sun. First, observe the way the wind blows, and then create a wind barrier perpendicular to the prevailing wind direction. This barrier can be a man-made wall or a row of evergreen trees. To encourage more sun to enter the house in winter, make sure you don't have any evergreen trees or shrubs obstructing the windows on the south side of your home.

678 In hot climates, leafy trees or vines can protect your house from the sun. In fact, a dense tree can block 75 percent of the sun's warmth. Be sure to shade your air conditioners too—they operate more efficiently out of direct sunlight. Avoid paved outdoor areas that retain heat and reflect glare back into your house.

679

In temperate zones with hot summers and very cold winter, carefully balance the landscape elements. If your bill for summer air conditioning is much higher than the winter heating bill, or vice versa, focus on your changing landscape to lessen the effects of weather during the more expensive seasons.

Wood floors—pickled or stained a light

or medium tone—wear well in kitchens

if once a year they are sanded with

steel wool and given a fresh coat of

polyurethane.

Choose materials that look good as they age— natural wood will mellow, figured limestone won't show stains, integral-color plaster never needs painting.

8 Entertaining Inside & Outside

Here are ideas about how to entertain with flair in both your indoor and outdoor spaces. Think of your front and backyards, porches and decks, balconies, and terraces as extensions of your home. If you are among the lucky few who have such space we have come up with tips and even recipes for making the most of your piece of the outdoors. Whether you are making a show-stopping garden party or need help putting together a memorable picnic, we have great advice.

If you lack for space outdoors we have creative ideas on how to bring the outdoors in. Create a garden inside your home with a floral tablecloth, or decorate a room with furniture made of organic materials and objects from nature. Brilliant entertaining can take place indoors and out—learn how to add just the right touches by draping fabrics, clustering candles, mixing tablewear, and playfully arranging your guests. Spruce up your rooms for the holidays or for any event. This is about celebrating you, your friends and family, and your home.

Tips for Brilliant Entertaining

682

Reinterpret recipes to make them your own.

683

Mix your porcelains on your table.

684

Invite at least one guest who's an expert in his or her field.

Heidi & Edward Killeen

PLEASE REPLY BY THE EIGHTH OF MARCH

WILL ATTEND

KINDLY RESPOND BY THE NINETEENTH OF JUNE

WILL ATTEND

Why:
When:
Where:
R.s.v.p.:

A Dinner Party

Please come for cocktails!!
May 20th at 6:00
House Beautiful
1700 Broadway
29th floor

685 *Guests adore surprise desserts.*

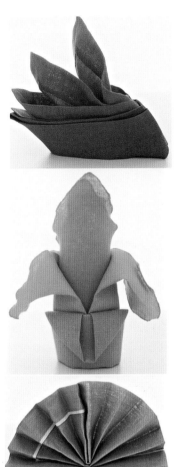

686 *Try using men's fine handker-chiefs instead of napkins.*

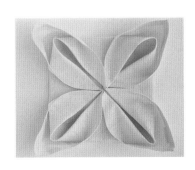

Transform an Everyday Area into a Show-Stopping Party Space

687

Illumination makes the mood. Up-lights gelled blue are cool; amber gels gain a warmer glow when diffused. Layers of tulle are great diffusers.

688

Always use lots of candles, from small, flickering votives to pillarlike church candles.

689

Offer a small party-themed gift to each guest.

600

Keep the time of day in mind. If decorations for your nighttime party look garish in full sun, remember that colors fade away when lights go down.

Draped fabric adds glamour to almost any event. It looks great on tables, furniture and even walls.

692

Here is a tip for a children's Halloween party: Chicken wire is an excellent material for creating shapes such as ghosts. After molding the figure, drape it in cheesecloth (another invaluable, cheap material), and then sponge the cheesecloth with fabric dyes to "personalize" the figure. Cut eyes and mouths out of felt and glue them on. If you want to hang the figure, use filament.

693

For centerpieces, use what's right outside your door, such as branches and leaves. Decorate them with spray paint and attach party-specific rubber figures and accent pieces from toy stores.

694

Buy lots of fabric such as tulle and use it to make a magical atmosphere.

695

Use floral spray and spray-paint in abundance, from coloring props to decorating temporary walls.

Flea markets and junk shops are good sources for cast-off props

and chairs that can be spray-painted or swathed in fabric

according to your party's theme.

697 Sometimes outdoor parties should be casual. Cover picnic tables with brown burlap tablecloths; even your best china will look terrific on them. Place beer in ice-filled terra-cotta tubs and let guests serve themselves.

698 Encourage down-home attire to loosen the mood.

699 Skimp on decorations and food if you must, but always have music— preferably live.

700 Big, high-spirited parties should always include children; tell each of them to invite a friend.

701 Oversize plates and large, heavy glasses make for unfussy eating and drinking.

702 Simple "found" table decorations can be enchanting. For example, heap peppers and limes in pretty bowls and decorate serving trays with flowers or leaves.

703 Arrange branches or wide variegated rocks on the table with candles interspersed among them.

For an uncomplicated buffet table,

arrange a single type of flower in simple

glass cylinders.

Prepare as much

as you can

ahead of time so

you can also

enjoy the party!

Entertain New Holiday Decorating Ideas

706
Hang a Christmas tree upside down. String a wire through a hole drilled sideways into the tree trunk. Tie the wire to a hook anchored into the ceiling.

707
Use a three-tired glass cake stand as a table centerpiece. Use all white desserts: white chocolate-covered pretzels, meringue cookies, and a tower of hand-made marshmallows on top.

708
On top of a single toned tablecloth, scatter handfuls of pearlescent petals and Lucite crystals.

Corral all your candlesticks in one spot.

Gather clear glass votives on a baking tray,

tucking mounds of moss around them.

Lace the tree with clear and frosted

white lights. Misting will keep it fresh for

two weeks.

712

Decorate with

fruit—it's less

perishable and

more economical

than flowers.

Any object from nature— the humblest

acorns or branches of bittersweet —can be

a centerpiece.

Wallpaper from the hardware store makes an

inexpensive wrapping.

Strings of fairy lights criss-crossed trellis-style a few inches beneath the ceiling, intertwined with ivy can transform a foyer.

Christmas crackers encourage fun at any party gathering. Buy inexpensive crackers to re-cover with hand-painted motifs—after stuffing them with upgraded gifts chosen for each guest.

Decorate with wrapped presents on a mantel.

Don't dismiss carnations. They smell wonderful and last longer than any other cut flowers.

Suspend a magnolia wreath from the ceiling.

Decorate a menorah with moss.

Decorating
Outdoor
Spaces

721

Even though it is temptingly inexpensive, resist the urge to use plastic furniture. After all, cheap plastic furniture is cheap and plastic.

722

Avoid glass tops on metal-framed outdoor tables—they're magnets for dirt. Use stone or painted-wood tops instead.

723

Make removable pillow covers with printed beach towels and Velcro.

One solid antique garden bench can make a world of difference

in an outdoor space.

For a sturdy option, teak is the best bet. It can handle the elements and acquires a silvery gray patina that grows lovelier the longer it's left outside.

Personalize outdoor furniture with custom cushions made of weather-resistant fabrics such as Sunbrella, Dralon, or Giati; fill them with quick-drying urethane foam that resists mildew. Pipe cushions in a contrasting color. White with black piping is classic—but pink piped with chocolate brown is chic.

Unify a motley collection of furniture by

painting pieces the same color. Painted

vintage metal furniture also weathers

storms and ages gracefully.

Try decorating with outdoor lanterns. Find old ones made of tin or painted wood, and store them in the mudroom when they're not being used.

Lightweight wicker, rattan, or bamboo pieces are not only historic favorites, they move easily to a covered porch or indoors in inclement weather.

Umbrellas add oomph to your garden, whether it's a fancy thatched palapa or a colorful and inexpensive plastic number.

No arrangement needs to be permanent. Move planters and furniture around as often as you like.

Treat outside like inside decorate with paintings, sculpture, even sofas and table lamps—sheltered by an awning or roof overhang.

The Keys to Outdoor Entertaining

733

Choose a date. If it falls near a holiday, confer with friends to avoid travel conflicts. If you are honoring someone, find two or three dates that suit the honoree first. If the group is large, call guests to reserve the date, then follow up with invitations, which should include pertinent information such as date, place, time, and specifics about attire.

734

Consider group dynamics. You want to stimulate conversation and avoid faux pas.

Please join us
for a Cajun dinner
under the August moon
at Greendune
Saturday, August 4,
2001
8 p.m.

Select a theme. Birthdays and anniversaries are obvious, but why not celebrate the height of fresh corn season?

For outdoor dinners, make sure you have plenty of bug spray, charcoal, lighter fluid, and citronella candles. And always have a backup in case of rain.

Prepare in advance as much as you can, from choosing table linens to renting chairs and hiring servers, cooks, and bartenders for larger parties.

When the entertainment (if any) arrives, discuss the flow of the evening with them as well as the musical selections.

Establish how many perishables —fresh flowers, plants, fruits, and vegetables—you'll need, and schedule an appropriate time to pick them up.

Three days before the dinner do nonperishable grocery shopping, leaving items such as fish, bread, and lettuce until the day of the party.

741 Arrange large floral centerpieces the day before, smaller bouquets the day of the party.

742 Prepare stocks, marinades, and pastry dough the day before. The day of, review menus, begin food preparation, set tables, add decorations, place the seating, bring beverages to appropriate temperatures, and set out the bar.

743 Get ready to greet your guests and have fun!

Bringing the Outdoors In

To encourage the use of a backyard or outdoor space, it helps to create a graceful and inviting transition from within the home to its exterior. The materials used in the room are essential to the success of the endeavor.

Large glass doors or oversize windows if left bare or dressed in the gauziest curtains or lace—let the light stream through and make the outside the focus.

746

Straw hats, baskets, botanical prints

and flower arrangements displayed

near doors and windows suggest the

natural delights that await you

outdoors.

The view to the outdoors from within is

important—French doors provide an open

invitation into the garden.

A flooring material such as flagstone or brick that easily makes the transition from indoors to out is a good starting point.

Garden and Picnic Entertaining—

Sweet and savory sandwich

sensations

Grilled Chicken and Arugula on a Baguette

4 skinless breasts of chicken marinated 2 hours in olive oil,
    crushed garlic, fresh thyme, rosemary, and crushed red pepper.

1 bottle good-quality cocktail sauce

4 baguette rolls, sliced in half horizontally

2 bunches arugula

1 3-ounce can of hot piquillos peppers

2 tomatoes, thinly sliced
    Salt and freshly ground black pepper

Remove chicken from the marinade. Discard marinade. Grill until cooked through, about 10 minutes per side. Set aside until cool. Slice each breast lengthwise into 2 pieces. Coat pieces with cocktail sauce. Set aside.

Spread 1/2 tablespoon cocktail sauce on each half of the roll. Layer arugula, peppers, tomatoes, and chicken on the bottom half of the bun. Repeat layering. Place the top of the bun on the sandwich. Repeat with remaining ingredients. *Serves 4.*

Brandade Sandwich with Cucumber and Radish Salad

1 bunch radishes, sliced 1/8 inch thick

1 cucumber, peeled, seeded and sliced 1/8 inch thick

2 tablespoons minced chives

3 tablespoons low-fat yogurt

   Juice of 2 lemons

16 Boston lettuce leaves

8 slices of rye bread

1 cup brandade, recipe follows

   Salt and freshly ground white pepper

Mix together radishes, cucumber, chives, yogurt, and lemon juice in a bowl. Set aside.

Place 2 lettuce leaves on a slice of bread. Top with a layer of radish and cucumber salad. Spread 2 tablespoons of brandade over salad. Top with salad, 2 lettuce leaves, salt and pepper to taste. Cover with a slice of bread. Repeat process with remaining ingredients. *Serves 4.*

Brandade

2 cups heavy cream

1/2 pound peeled garlic

1 pound Idaho potatoes, peeled and quartered

2 pounds boneless salted cod, soaked in water for 48 hours, water changed at least 4 times

1 quart milk

3 sprigs fresh thyme

2 sprigs fresh rosemary

2 whole garlic heads, sliced in half

1/2 to 1 cup extra-virgin olive oil

   salt and freshly ground white pepper to taste

   cayenne pepper

Heat heavy cream and peeled garlic in a saucepan over moderate heat until cream is reduced by half. Set aside.

Place potatoes in a saucepan, cover with water and bring to a boil. Cook until tender. Drain. Mash potatoes in a bowl. Set aside.

Place fish in a shallow pan. Add milk, thyme, rosemary, garlic heads, and enough water to completely submerge fish. Bring liquid to a simmer over moderate heat. Cook until done, about 8 minutes. Do not overcook. Remove fish with a slotted spoon and place in a food processor. Add mashed potatoes and cream. Process until lightly mixed. Place in a bowl. Add oil until mixture is creamy. Add salt, pepper, and cayenne to taste. *Makes about 1 1/2 cups.*

Bayaldi of Vegetables on Toasted Country Bread

4 tablespoons black olive paste (tapenade)
4 1/2-inch-thick slices of country bread, toasted on both sides
   Bayaldi of vegetables, recipe follows
8 1/2-inch-thick slices of fresh goat cheese
8 green or black pitted olives

Spread 1 tablespoon olive paste on a slice of bread. Arrange bayaldi of vegetables on top. Place 2 slices of goat cheese over vegetables. Place an olive on top of each piece of goat cheese. Place sandwich on a baking sheet. Repeat process with other ingredients.

   Bake in a preheated 450°F oven until sandwiches are warm and cheese has lightly melted, about 3 minutes. Remove pan from oven. *Serves 4.*

Bayaldi of Vegetables

1 Spanish onion, peeled and thinly sliced
2 cloves garlic, peeled and minced
1 teaspoon chopped fresh thyme
1 teaspoon chopped fresh rosemary
4 yellow plum tomatoes, sliced 1/2 inch thick
4 red plum tomatoes, sliced 1/2 inch thick
2 yellow squash, sliced 1/2 inch thick
2 zucchini, sliced 1/2 inch thick
2 Japanese eggplants, sliced ? inch thick
   olive oil
   salt and freshly ground white pepper

Place a thin layer of onions on the bottom of an 8"x10" earthenware dish. Sprinkle half the garlic, thyme, and rosemary on top. Working lengthwise, alternate tomatoes, squash, zucchini, and eggplant slices until a row is complete. Repeat the process until all the vegetables are used. Brush a liberal amount of olive oil on top layer. Sprinkle with remaining garlic and herbs. Season with salt and pepper to taste. Cover dish with aluminum foil and bake in a preheated 350°F oven for 1 1/2 hours. Baste with olive oil every 15 minutes. Remove foil the last 1/2 hour of cooking. Remove pan from oven. Let vegetables stand 20 minutes before using.

Pain Bagnat

Mustard dressing, recipe follows

  4 *loaves pan bagnat or white bread rolls, sliced in half*
      horizontally
 12 *Boston lettuce leaves*
  2 *tomatoes, sliced*
  2 *hard-boiled eggs, sliced*
  3 *bell peppers (red, yellow, and green), cored, seeded, and cut*
      into strips
  2 *scallions, trimmed and chopped*
  1 *cup fresh basil leaves*
  2 *radishes, thinly sliced*
      salt and freshly ground black pepper
 12 *ounces canned white tuna, drained*
  8 *Niçoise olives, pitted*
  8 *flat anchovy filets*

Generously drizzle mustard dressing on both halves of the bread.
Set aside.

Place 3 lettuce leaves on the bottom slice. Layer with tomato,
egg, pepper strips, scallions, basil leaves, and radishes. Season with
salt, pepper, and dressing to taste. Arrange tuna over vegetables
and season to taste. Place reserved bread slice on top. Skewer a
toothpick with 2 olives and 2 anchovies. Repeat process with
remaining ingredients. *Serves 4.*

Mustard Dressing

 1 *cup red wine vinegar*
 2 *teaspoons salt*
 1 *teaspoon freshly ground black pepper*
 4 *tablespoons Dijon mustard*
 4 *cups extra-virgin olive oil*

Whisk vinegar, salt, pepper, and mustard in a mixing bowl. Slowly
whisk in oil. *Makes 5 cups.*

Croque Monsieur

Béchamel sauce, recipe follows

8   1-inch-thick slices of white bread, toasted on both sides
8   slices Swiss cheese
4   slices ham
5   cups grated Swiss cheese

Spread 1 tablespoon of béchamel sauce on a slice of toast. Place a slice of cheese and a slice of ham over sauce. Top with a slice of toast. Spread top of toast with 1 tablespoon béchamel sauce. Place sandwich on a baking sheet. Cover sandwich with about 1 1/2 cups grated cheese. Repeat process with remaining ingredients.

Place baking sheet on center of rack in the broiler. Broil in a preheated 500°F broiler until cheese is golden brown. *Serves 4.*

Béchamel Sauce

2 1/2   tablespoons butter
 1/2   cup pastry flour
  2   cups milk, heated
  6   tablespoons grated Swiss cheese
      salt, freshly ground white pepper, nutmeg, and cayenne
      pepper to taste

Melt butter in a heavy saucepan over low heat. Add flour and cook, stirring constantly, until flour is completely incorporated, about 2 minutes. Remove pan from heat. Whisk in milk until mixture is smooth. Place pan over moderately high heat. Bring to a boil, stirring constantly, about 3 minutes. Remove pan from heat. Add remaining ingredients. Stir until cheese has melted. *Makes about 2 1/2 cups.*

Herbed Rotisserie Chicken (see recipe on page 430)

Dining Alfresco— Garden Gourmet

749

Put food on big platters and toss flowers and herbs around the edges and on the table to decorate.

750

Cold food needs more seasoning than hot food— the cold temperature suppresses the flavors.

Chilled Beet and Cucumber Soup

8 *medium beets, trimmed and washed*

1 *tablespoon butter*

1 *large Spanish onion, peeled and finely chopped*

1 *large carrot, peeled and finely chopped*

1 *tablespoon sugar*

4 *cups chicken or vegetable stock*

3 *tablespoons red wine vinegar*

  Salt and freshly ground black pepper

1 1/2 *cups sour cream or yogurt*

2 *tablespoons chopped chives*

3 *tablespoons finely chopped dill*

1 *unwaxed European cucumber, grated*

Wrap beets in heavy-duty aluminum foil and bake in preheated 375° F oven for about 1 hour, or until tender when pierced with a fork. When beets are cool enough to handle, remove skins and cut in half. Set aside.

Place the butter in a large sauté pan and set over medium heat. Add onions and carrots and sauté until onions are translucent. Add beets, sugar, and stock, and simmer for 20 minutes. Remove pan from heat. Set aside for 15 minutes.

Place beet mixture and vinegar in a food processor and purée. Season with salt and pepper to taste. Pour into a pitcher. Chill. Stir in sour cream, chives, chopped dill, and cucumber. Serve in wine-glasses. *Serves 6.*

Herbed Rotisserie Chicken

1/2 cup chopped flat-leaf parsley

3 cloves garlic, chopped finely

*   Juice of 2 lemons*

3 tablespoons olive oil

2 free-range chickens, 3 to 3 1/2 pounds each, rinsed and dried

2 sprigs each of thyme, rosemary, and sage

*   salt and freshly ground black pepper*

Mix together in a bowl parsley, garlic, lemon juice, and olive oil. Refrigerate at least 1 hour or overnight.

Light a wood-burning rotisserie and stoke fire until ready to cook without flaming.

Remove chickens from the refrigerator. Place a sprig of thyme, rosemary, and sage in each cavity. Salt and pepper inside and out. Tie the legs together with kitchen twine.

Thread chickens on rotisserie. Cook over fire for approximately 1 1/2 hours, or until a needle inserted in the thick part of the leg produces clear juices.

Transfer chickens to a large serving platter. Allow to rest at least 15 minutes before carving. Serve warm or at room temperature. *Serves 6.*

Fried Zucchini Blossoms

1 cup Wondra superfine flour

1/2 teaspoon salt plus salt for seasoning

*   ice water*

*   vegetable oil*

12 zucchini blossoms with stems

Place flour and salt in a bowl. Whisk in enough ice water to make the batter the consistency of heavy cream. Set aside.

Heat 2 to 3 inches of oil in a cast-iron skillet until almost smoking. Dip 4 to 5 blossoms in the batter and shake off any excess. Fry for about 1 minute on each side, or until golden. Remove with a slotted spoon and drain on paper towels. Sprinkle with salt. Repeat process with remaining blossoms. Serve immediately. *Serves 6.*

Tomatoes Provençale

3 tablespoons extra-virgin olive oil

6 tablespoons fresh bread crumbs

   salt

   sugar

12 small or 6 large whole vine-ripened tomatoes

3 garlic cloves, peeled and chopped fine

3 tablespoons chopped flat-leaf parsley

   calendula petals or other edible flowers, optional

Mix 1 tablespoon olive oil and bread crumbs together in a bowl. Spread mixture on a parchment-lined baking sheet. Bake in a pre-heated 350°F oven for about 15 minutes, stirring frequently, or until bread crumbs are brown. Remove pan from oven. Set aside.

Slice off the stem ends of the tomatoes, and squeeze gently to remove the seeds. Discard seeds. Set aside.

Add 1 tablespoon olive oil to a cast-iron or enamel pan. Heat oil over medium heat until almost smoking. Lightly salt and sugar tomatoes and place cut side down in pan. Sear and cook until juices are released and bubbling. Turn tomatoes over gently.

Mix garlic and parsley together in a bowl. Spread mixture evenly over tops of tomatoes. Drizzle with remaining oil. Baste again with pan juices. Continue to cook and baste until tomatoes start to wrinkle and juices thicken. Spread bread crumbs over tomatoes. Baste again with pan juices. Place pan in a preheated 300°F oven and cook until tomatoes and juices have caramelized, about 30 minutes. Remove pan from oven. Garnish with calendula petals. Serve at room temperature. *Serves 6.*

Haricots Verts and Chanterelle Salad

1½ *pounds haricots verts, stem ends trimmed*

  2 *tablespoons extra-virgin olive oil*

  1 *large shallot, peeled and finely minced*

½ *pound chanterelle mushrooms, cleaned, chopped, and trimmed*

½ *cup chopped flat-leaf parsley*

    Dressing, recipe below

Blanch haricots verts in a large pot of salted boiling water for 1 minute, or until just tender. Plunge into a basin of ice-cold water. Drain and pat dry between layers of paper towels. Set aside.

Heat the oil in a large skillet over medium heat. Add shallots and sauté for 2 minutes. Raise heat to high, add mushrooms all at once, and quickly sauté, stirring constantly, about 3 to 5 minutes. Add parsley and lightly toss for 30 seconds. Remove pan from heat.

Place haricots verts in a serving platter and toss with dressing. Add mushrooms and toss again. *Serves 6.*

Dressing

  2 *tablespoons aged Spanish sherry vinegar*

    salt and freshly ground black pepper to taste

½ *cup extra-virgin olive oil*

Mix together vinegar, salt, and pepper in a bowl. Whisk in olive oil. Set aside. *Makes about ½ cup.*

Blackberries and Lemon Verbena Sabayon

6 egg yolks

3 tablespoons sugar

1/2 cup Sauterene, heated and infused with 12 lemon verbena leaves or 2 vervain tea bags

1 pint heavy cream, whipped

2 pints blackberries

Place egg yolks and sugar in the top of a double boiler over simmering water. Beat until thick and pale yellow, approximately 10 minutes.

Strain wine mixture. Discard leaves. Add wine and continue cooking, stirring constantly, until the mixture thickens enough to coat the back of a spoon. Remove the top of boiler from stove. Set over bowl of ice and continue beating until cool. Fold in cream. Serve with berries. Makes about 4 cups. *Serves 6.*

A Midsummer Night's Dream
A garden party in the spirit of a French picnic

Deviled Eggs

12 *large hard-boiled eggs, peeled*
 5 *tablespoons mayonnaise, preferably homemade*
     zest of 1 lemon
 2 *teaspoons chopped cilantro stems*
 1 *tablespoon Thai garlic chili sauce*
     sea salt
     mixed varieties of lettuce

Cut each egg in half lengthwise. Carefully remove yolks and place in the bowl of a food processor. Place egg whites on a serving platter. Set aside.

Add mayonnaise, lemon zest, cilantro stems, Thai garlic chili sauce, and salt to taste to bowl. Process until mixture is just smooth. Place in a pastry bag fitted with a star tip. Pipe a mound of yolk mixture into well of each egg white. Cover with plastic wrap. Refrigerate. Serve slightly chilled or at room temperature. Garnish platter with mixed lettuce leaves. *Makes 24.*

Mussels Escabeche

1 cup tomato juice

1 tomato peeled, seeded, and cut in to 1/2-inch dice (about 1/2 cup)

2 shallots, peeled and cut into 1/2-inch dice

1 medium red pepper, halved, seeded, and cut into 1/2-inch dice

1 medium yellow pepper, halved, seeded, and cut into 1/2-inch dice

1/2 jalapeño chili stemmed, seeded, and cut into 1/2-inch dice

1/2 cup fresh cilantro leaves, finely chopped

   juice of 1 lime

1 1/2 tablespoons seasoned rice wine vinegar

2 tablespoons extra-virgin olive oil

   sea salt

   freshly ground black pepper

3 pounds mussels, scrubbed, bearded, steamed, and top half of shells removed

   Lemon verbena leaves

Place tomato juice, diced vegetables, cilantro leaves, lime juice, vinegar, and olive oil in a bowl. Add salt and pepper to taste. Cover. Refrigerate 2 hours.

Arrange mussels on a large platter. (Mussels can be arranged, covered, and refrigerated several hours before serving.) Using a slotted spoon, top each mussel with vegetable mixture. Drizzle a small amount of juice from vegetables over mussels. Garnish platter with lemon verbena leaves. *Serves 12.*

Herb-Cured Niçoise Olives

1 cup Niçoise olives

1 cup picholine olives

2 tablespoons olive oil

1 clove garlic, peeled and slivered

1 teaspoon chopped, lavender flowers, fresh or dried

1 tablespoon chopped fresh chive blossoms

1 teaspoon chopped fresh thyme

   sea salt and freshly ground black pepper, to taste

   fresh thyme sprigs

Mix all ingredients, except thyme sprigs, in a bowl. Cover. Marinate 2 to 3 days. Drain. Serve olives in bowls. Garnish with thyme sprigs. *Makes about 2 cups.*

Tomato and Basil Salad

8 extra-large, vine-ripened beefsteak or heirloom tomatoes, tops
    and bottoms cut off
    sea salt
    basil leaves
    freshly ground black pepper

Cut each tomato into three slices. Salt each slice to taste. Overlap
slices on a platter. Place basil leaves between slices. Garnish center
of dish with extra basil leaves. Add pepper to taste. Set aside for
1/2 hour before serving. *Serves 12.*

Slow-Roasted Salmon

8 1/2-pound salmon fillets with skin, at room temperature
    extra-virgin olive oil
1 cup finely minced fresh chives
    sea salt and freshly ground white pepper
    fresh sage leaves

Lightly brush flesh of salmon fillets with olive oil. Completely
cover with chives and gently press into flesh. Season with salt and
pepper to taste. Place fillets skin-side-down on a non-stick or
slightly oiled foil-lined baking pan. Roast in a preheated 250°F
oven for 17 minutes. Place fillets on a serving dish. Serve at room
temperature. Garnish with sage sprigs. *Serves 8.*

Vegetable-Orzo Salad

sea salt

1 medium carrot, peeled, trimmed, and julienned on a mandoline

1 small celery root, peeled, trimmed, and julienned on a mandoline

2 small fennel bulbs, white part only, trimmed and julienned on a mandoline

1 4-inch long zucchini, trimmed and julienned on a mandoline

2 small leeks, white part only, thoroughly washed, trimmed, peeled and finely diced

1 red pepper, halved, cored, peeled, and finely diced

2 shallots, peeled and finely diced

2 sprigs fresh tarragon, finely chopped

1 bunch fresh chervil, finely chopped

1/2 cup mixed varieties of lettuce

1 pound orzo

3 tablespoons champagne vinegar

4 tablespoons extra-virgin olive oil

freshly ground black pepper

Place 2 cups salted water in a saucepan and bring to a boil. Add carrots and cook for 1 1/2 minutes. Remove pan from heat. Drain. Set aside. Repeat process with celery root, fennel, and zucchini. Cook zucchini in 1/2 minute. Finely dice each vegetable. Place in a bowl. Add leeks, red peppers, shallots, tarragon sprigs, chervil and lettuce. Cover. Set aside.

Place 2 quarts water in a large pot. Add 1 tablespoon salt. Bring to a boil. Add orzo and return to a boil. Cook until firm, about 12 minutes. Start checking for doneness after 10 minutes. Drain. Rinse under cold water. Place in a bowl.

Mix vinegar, oil, salt and pepper to taste in a bowl. Gently mix into orzo. Mix in diced vegetables. Set aside for about 1 hour, folding gently several times before serving. Serves 8.

Grilled Free-Range Chicken Breasts with Saffron Aioli

3 *tablespoons extra-virgin olive oil*

1 *lemon, washed and sliced lengthwise in to 8 pieces*

2 *cloves garlic, peeled and slivered*

1 *shallot, peeled and slivered*

1 *teaspoon herbes de Provence*

   freshly ground black pepper

8 *chicken breasts, wing bones removed*

   sea salt

   saffron aioli, recipe follows

Mix olive oil, lemon slices, garlic, shallots, herbs, and pepper to taste together in a bowl. Place chicken breasts in a glass dish. Add marinade. Cover. Marinate in refrigerator for at least 4 hours, turning several times.

Remove dish form refrigerator. Remove chicken breasts from marinade. Reserve marinade. Season with salt to taste. Cook skinside-down on a preheated hot grill until charred, about 5 minutes. Rotate 90 degrees for cross-hatched grill marks. Cook about 4 minutes. Turn over, brush with reserved marinade, and cook until done, about 2 minutes. Meat should remain moist. Do not overcook. Remove from grill. Cut each chicken breast crosswise at a 45-degree angle into ?-inch-thick pieces. Arranged fanned out on a dinner plate. Serve with a generous spoonful of saffron aioli. *Serves 8.*

Saffron Aioli

 3 *cloves garlic, peeled*

1/8 *teaspoon sea salt*

 2 *large egg yolks*

1/2 *teaspoon Spanish saffron threads soaked in 1 tablespoon*

   warm water for 40 minutes

 1 *cup extra-virgin olive oil*

 2 *tablespoons fresh lemon juice*

   freshly ground black pepper

Grind garlic and salt into a paste with a mortar and pestle. Mix in egg yolks and saffron mixture. Gradually whisk in half of the olive oil until mixture just begins to thicken. Add 1 tablespoon lemon juice. Whisk in remaining oil. Do not overbeat. Mix in remaining lemon juice. Add pepper too taste. *Makes about 11/2 cups.*

Three Bean Salad with Sage and Thyme Vinaigrette

1 cup dried flageolet beans, soaked overnight in water to cover and refrigerated

1 cup dried cannellini beans, soaked overnight in water to cover and refrigerated

1 1/2 pounds haricot verts, ends trimmed
    Sea salt

2 small celery stalks, leaves discarded, diced 1/2-inch thick

3 kirby cucumbers, peeled, seeded, and diced 1/2-inch-thick

2 large sweet yellow peppers, roasted, skinned, seeded, and finely diced

6 thin scallions, white part only, cut into thin rings
    sage and thyme vinaigrette, recipe follows
    thyme flowers
    sage leaves
    freshly ground black pepper

Remove flageolet and cannellini beans from refrigerator. Drain. Place flageolet and cannelloni beans in separate pots. Cover with 3 inches of water. Bring to a boil over medium heat. Skim any foam that rises. Reduce heat to simmer. Partially cover the pots. Simmer cannellini beans, stirring occasionally, until tender, about 45 minutes. Simmer flageolet beans, stirring occasionally until tender, about 1 hour. Add more water if necessary. Drain. Set aside.

Place a large pot of salted water over medium heat and bring to a boil. Add haricots verts and cook until just tender, about 5 minutes. Drain. Plunge into ice water. Drain. Cut into 1/2-inch pieces.

Place beans, diced vegetables, and scallion rings in a bowl. Toss with vinaigrette. Add salt and pepper to taste. Serve at room temperature. Garnish with thyme flowers and sage leaves. *Makes about 8 cups.*

Sage and Thyme Vinaigrette

8 tablespoons extra-virgin olive oil

2 tablespoons champagne vinegar
    juice of 1 lemon

8 fresh sage leaves, finely chopped

2 tablespoons chopped fresh thyme leaves
    freshly ground black pepper

Whisk together oil, vinegar, and lemon juice in a bowl. Mix in sage and thyme leaves, salt and pepper to taste. *Makes about 1/2 cups.*

Lemon-Lime Possent

    4 cups heavy cream
1 2/3 cups superfine sugar
        juice of 3 lemons and 2 key limes or 4 lemons
        crème fraiche
        fresh mint leaves
        pound cake

Place heavy cream and sugar in a stainless steel pan. Bring to a
boil. Cook 3 minutes, stirring constantly. Remove pan from heat.
Thoroughly mix in lemon and lime juice. Cool for 5 minutes. Pour
mixture into 8 one-cup chilled glasses. Refrigerate until set, about
3 hours. Remove from refrigerator. Garnish with crème fraiche and
mint leaves. Serve with pound cake. *Serves 8.*

Photo Credits

Peter Aaron/Esto: 356

Melanie Acevedo: 233, 299

Francis Amiand: 104, 195, 276

Sang An: 3 (bottom), 137, 140, 145, 163
    (bottom), 285 (top), 379

Bruch Archibald: 92 (bottom)

Quentin Bacon: 414, 422-23, 432-33,
    440-41

Alexandre Bailhache: 126 (bottom),
    154-55, 213, 230,

Edmund Barr: top 16, 161, 226-27,
    264-65,

Gordon Beall: 298

Tim Beddow: 23 (bottom), 40-1,
    43-5, 78-9

Fernando Bengoechea: 62-3, 144

Eric Boman: top 24, 60-1, 72-3, 80, 85,
    160 (bottom), 166, 174-75, 248-49,
    254-55, 279, 286-87, 350-51, 357,
    358-59, 378, 394-98, 419

Antoine Bootz: 34-5, 36-7, 120-21, 268
    (bottom), 274-5, 328

Gracia Branco: 199, 209

Langdon Clay: 7 (bottom), 186, 192-93,
    284, 418

John Coolidge: 101

Paul Costello: 324-5, 327, 391

Susie Cushner: 55, 296-97

Beatriz DaCosta: 379 (top left)

Lisl Dennis: 303

Carlos Domenech: 273

Jacques Dirand: 25 (top), 83 (bottom),
    158-9, 380

Miki Duisterhof: 286

Michael Dunne: 178-79, 206-07, 416-
    17, 424-25

Tom Eckerle: 64

John Ellis: 110-111

Carlos Emilio: 56, 188-89, 208 (top),
    269, 281-83, 412-13

Pieter Estersohn: 29, 340

Richard Felber: 152-53, 259, 290 (top),
    291 (bottom), 338-39, 350 (top),
    436-39

Feliciano: 253

Lendon Flanagan: bottom 16, 73, 148
    (top), 175-76

Scott Frances: 8-9, 52, 102-3, 115,
    196-97, 200-05, 308-09

Dana Gallagher: 27 (bottom), 57 (top),
    58, 61, 64 (top), 69, 94-5, 183 (left),
    208 (bottom), 304-05, 426-27

David George: 381

Oberto Gili: 13-5, 18, 54-5, 68-9, 105,
    126 (top), 134-35, 141, 168
    (bottom), 177, 182, 212 (bottom),
    245, 261, 270-71, 310-11, 347, 393,
    417, 420-21

David Glomb: 164

Jeff Goldberg/Esto: 122-23

Sam Gray: 128-33

Anne Gummerson: 86-7

Kari Haavisto: 123

Matthew Harnek: 409

Alec Hemer: 330-31

Robert Hiemstra: 211, 348-49

Lizzie Himmel: 173, 237

Lisa Hubbard: 434-35

Timothy Hursley: 165

Jean Francois Jaussaud: 184, 210,
    220 (top)

Thibault Jeanson: 8-9, 18-21, 66-7, 92
    (top), 127, 148 (bottom), 168 (top),
    217, 243, 256, 300-01, 404, 406

Jon Jensen: 90, 108-9, 113, 360-61

Andrew Lawson: 184-85

Stephen Lewis: 95 (top), 98 (bottom)

David Duncan Livingston: 118-9

Peter Margonelli: 89, 107, 138, top 268,
    326, 332-33

Nedjeljko Matura: 22 (bottom), 25
    (bottom right), 81, 139 (bottom),
    149 (top), 228-29, 260 (top), 285
    (bottom)

Elizabeth Mayhew: 290

Simon McBride: 172

Tom McCavera: 35

Ericka McConnell: 403, 408

Jason McConathy: 57 (bottom), 260
    (bottom), 277

Maura McEvoy: 98 (top)

Jeff McNamara: 49, 162, top 163, 215,
    218-19, 232, 405

Tom McWilliam: 93, 216, top 291, 320,
    342, 362-63

Minh & Wass: center 51, 142-43, 167

Molly's Folly: top 27,

Michael O'Brien: 329, 407

Victoria Pearson: 28, 100, 187 (bottom),
    198, 331 (top), 354-55

Laura Resen: 246-47, 319 (bottom), 334

Lisa Romerin: 169

Eric Roth: 50-1, 82, 194-95, 221,
    240-41, 352-53

Mark Samu: 371

Jeremy Samuelson: top 160, 280

Joshua Sheldon: top 3, 23, 24 (bottom),
    51(top and bottom), 183 (right), 187
    (top), 331 (bottom), 341, (bottom
    350), 353, 364

Christopher Simon Sykes: 96-7

Walter Smalling: 368-69

Margherita Spiluttini: 368

Robert Starkoff: 258-59

Hugh Stewart: 428-29

Tim Street-Porter: 26-7, 99, 225 (right),
    256-57, 266-67, 336-7, 367

Rene Stoeltie: top 22, 42, 181, 305

Buff Strickland: 106-7, 114 (top),
    115-6, 387

Stefan Studer: 70-1, 220 (bottom), 224,
    225 (left), 293 (top), 399 (top),
    410-11, 411 (top), 415

Luca Trovato: 95(bottom), 321-23, 371

Pia Tryde: 38-9, 386-87

Simon Upton: 30-2, 83 (top), 112,
    190-91, 212(top), 222-23, 264, 278,
    356 (top), 392, 401

John Vaughan: 364-65

Dominique Vorillon: 46-7, 139 (top),
    314-15, 317, 366

William Waldron: 7 (top), 53, 74-7,
    88-9, 90-1, 170-71, 231, 239, 242,
    255, 306-07, 316 (top), 335 (top),
    355, 358, 390-91, 400

Simon Watson: 289, 293(bottom), 294
    (top), 295

Jonelle Weaver: 430-31

Michael Weschler: 59, 114 (bottom),

Paul Whicheloe: 25 (bottom left), 149
    (bottom), 159, 319 (top), 335 (bottom)

Luke White: 64-5, 146-47, 150

Jack Winston: 288, 338

Vincente Wolf: 312-13

Gabi Zimmerman: 150-51

Index